LESLEY ELDER

I Would Rather Eat a Cactus...than Run a Project

For Roque, my rock.

Contents

Foreword   iii

  Who Is This Book For?   iii

  Who am I and How Did I Get Here?   vi

Acknowledgement   xii

1 Project Initiation   1

  What Is a Project?   1

  The Project Governance Process   5

  Ideas   5

  The Ideas Funnel   6

  The Project Investment Board   12

2 The Business Case & Project Charter   17

  The Business Case   17

  The Project Charter   21

3 Kicking Off the Project   24

  Resourcing the Project & Assembling the
Team   24

  The Kick-off Workshop   26

4 Project Roles   32

  Key Project Roles   32

  Chapter 4 Summary - What Have We
Learned?   48

5 The Project Management Plan   49

6 Business Readiness, Communications &
    Training Plans   80

7   Risk Management & The RAID Log   103

8   Executing the Project   113

9   Closing the Project   127

10   Monitoring & Controlling the Project   135

11   Agile Project Management   141

12   Bonus Section – Change Behaviours   156

13   Acronyms   166

14   Glossary   168

Foreword

Welcome to my book! If you are looking for practical insights into the confusing and jargon-filled world of projects, then you are in exactly the right place! My intention is to share with you my knowledge and experience and give you an introduction to the basics. Armed with that, you will be able to confidently explore everything that the world of project management has to offer.

However, before we go any further let's get one thing clear. This is not a project management textbook. If you are looking for a detailed step-by-step guide on how to become a Project Manager, unfortunately, you have come to the wrong place. There are loads of excellent manuals out there that will give you that training, but this isn't one of them.

Who Is This Book For?

This book is aimed primarily at the uninitiated. People who haven't worked on a project before, or who have completed a project management training course but have yet to put their knowledge into practice. It's not really aimed at seasoned Project Managers, although you are very welcome here. And if you stick around, I expect there to be some nodding and the odd chuckle as you recognise some familiar scenarios.

Do you see yourself in one of the following examples?:

Complete Newbies – Your boss has asked you to do a project for the first time and you're not trained in project management. You have no idea where to start, and you don't even know what you don't know. This book will explain the basics.

Secondees/Subject Matter Experts (SMEs) – You normally work in another area, but you've been asked to provide input to a project, or worse, you've been "seconded" from your current job onto a project team, and you feel like the Project Manager is speaking a different language. Think of this book as your translator.

Recruiters – Someone has asked you to hire a Project Manager, or a Business Change Manager or a Business Analyst. And you don't really understand the difference between the roles and what skills are required for each one. It's all in here.

Auditors – You normally look at company accounts and governance processes. You've been asked to do a risk assessment of a project and, other than going through the checklist you've been given, you're not really sure what to look for. Do not fear, this book will help.

Career Movers and Shakers – Your boss has suggested that the best way for you to get promoted is 'to get some project experience'. Eeek! You don't know the first thing about projects.

iv

This book will help you figure out where to start and what not to do, without converting you into a full-time Project Manager.

Project Management Students – You've done the course, you've got your shiny, new project management certificate, and you're ready to be unleashed into an unsuspecting world. Except you're not quite sure where to start. You don't have any experience. And it's all starting to feel a little bit different from what you learned in your course. This book will help by giving you the benefit of my twenty-plus years of experience, helping you to find your feet and get started on your first "real world" project.

Career Changers – You've seen people go off to work on projects and it looks fun. Much more interesting than doing the same thing day in, day out. And you want to find out a bit more before putting your hand up. This book will give you a flavour of what it's really like to work on a project.

Function Specialists, e.g. Finance, HR, Legal, Risk – Your new role is to provide support to projects, and you haven't got a clue how they work, who does what, or how you can help. Do not worry, help is at hand. This book will give you the basics and help you figure out how to support your new best friends, the Project Managers. And, better yet, help you to get the information you need from them!

Volunteers in Charity or Not-for-Profit Organisations – You're keen to get involved and have a big impact, there's little funding available, and everyone has a different idea about how to get the new project off the ground. This book can help to create a common starting point, getting everyone on the same page, and creating a foundation for the approach to managing your change or project. It can also help to explain why things need to be done in a structured way when the urge is to just start, to just do something.

Project Management Professionals – This book doesn't go into every aspect of project management in the detail you will be used to. That's not what it's for. But you may find it entertaining, recognising similar situations as they arise throughout the book. And what you may find useful is being able to share it with the members of your new project team, so that you are all, literally, on the same page. At the very least, it will save you from having to explain the difference between a 'risk' and an 'issue' for 42nd millionth time.

If you can relate to any of the situations above, then this is definitely the book for you. Read on for excellent tips, constructive help, and practical examples of how to make your project experience easier.

Who am I and How Did I Get Here?

If you're still here, then let me introduce myself properly and tell you how this book came about.

I've worked in project management for most of my career, but it came about by accident. I didn't leave school and think 'oh, I want to be a Project Manager'. Like most teenagers I wouldn't have known that such a job even existed.

I joined a graduate scheme in banking at the ripe old age of twenty-six...I was quite late in getting to university, but that's a story for another book! As part of my graduate training programme, I worked in local branches learning what banking was all about from the ground up. I would thoroughly recommend this approach to anyone leaving university, as that basic knowledge gave me foundations that would later serve me well. There's no substitute for knowing why things are done a certain way.

In my naivety, I took the bold step of writing to our regional manager suggesting a few things that could be done differently to make some of the branch processes more efficient. He was the only person I knew in the head office, and when I initially met him in the branch, he seemed like a pleasant man. I hoped he would be open to my suggestions for improvement.

The next thing I knew, I was being summoned into the head office in the city. Eek! Was I about to get fired for my cheekiness? Would they laugh me out of the building? Thankfully not. They weren't particularly overwhelmed by my suggestions; the problems were well known but would be costly to fix. But they were impressed by the fact that I had taken the initiative to point out that things could be improved. They then offered me the chance to transfer into the head office projects team and learn how to tackle process improvement. I jumped at the chance to learn something new and waved goodbye to my short-lived branch career.

And this began my introduction into the world of project management. My new boss quickly pulled together a training plan for me which involved a series of rotations around the different project disciplines. It soon became apparent that I didn't have the patience or attention span for business analysis and that process improvement didn't really interest me, despite my initial branch findings (more on these topics later). But project management? Organising everyone and getting things done? I had found my calling.

Over the next twenty years, I was lucky enough to be involved in all types of projects, but always within banking, pensions, or other financial services businesses. However, that lack of industry diversity never bothered me. The basics of project management never change, and it's a discipline that provides loads of transferable skills.

Early on in my career, I enjoyed being a hands-on Project Manager, getting the chance to find out about things I would never have become involved in otherwise. From how a bank addresses the issue of mortgage mis-selling (start a remediation project), to whether to outsource call service work to India or not (send a project team to investigate). And how to get an entire bank to comply with new banking regulations (or not!).

I eventually found myself in interim Head of Change or Head of Projects roles, stepping in when things weren't going well, or when the business needed someone to hold the fort while they recruited a permanent replacement. This gave me the opportunity to shift my focus from purely delivering projects to managing teams of Project Managers, Business Asnalyst, and PMO teams.

As I continued to build my interim and consultancy business, the introduction of new tax regulations in the UK made it more difficult for organisations to hire independent consultants like me. I decided that I needed to do something to stand out from the crowd and set about updating my LinkedIn profile. I re-focused and started posting on topics that were close to my heart.

One of these topics was the complete lack of understanding of project roles by some recruiters. Junior agency staff who had been told to find candidates for roles that they didn't understand and had little experience recruiting for. It wasn't their fault. The business model they had been hired into had become increasingly competitive and relied on a 'first past the post' approach. Whoever could get some vaguely suitable candidates into the lap of the hiring manager first had the best chance of taking some commission from placing a candidate they barely knew.

I fielded many calls from these poor unsuspecting individuals. I especially enjoyed those where they called me about a completely unsuitable role such as a Business Analyst position. Little did they know they would be getting an education about the difference between a Project Manager and a Business Analyst when they called me up.

But trying to educate them one by one wasn't going to solve the broader problem, so I decided a better plan of attack would be to start posting some of the basics on my LinkedIn profile. Because this is where most of them initially found me, so they must be paying attention, right? I set out to explain project management for the uninitiated, including the difference between project roles, and what a project cost plan is.

At the same time, I was conscious that, on several occasions in my career, I had failed on a very important project management principle—never assume! As an interim manager taking on a new project team, I would assume that they 'knew the basics' and that everyone was on the same page. This was not always the case. Project Managers who didn't know how to create a cost plan, PMO Analysts who didn't know what a Gantt chart was (don't worry, I will explain these later!) and much more.

The challenge with this group is that they are scared to ask the questions. Because they should know this stuff by now, right? I saw it time and again, and I had a hunch that there was more of this going on than you would think.

I wanted to tackle this in a way that people could dip into without fear of embarrassment. And do you know what? My hunch was right. As soon as I started my 'project jargon' posts, I had lots of messages sent saying 'thanks for explaining that', or asking me about things that the sender thought they should already know but were now too far into their new job to ask.

The interesting thing about this is that they wouldn't post these comments or questions on the actual LinkedIn post. They were always in private messages!

The audience for my posts expanded to include those people who were too embarrassed to speak up (see Chapter 6 for more on this). And perhaps also to make my peers nod and have a bit of a chuckle. Because they know what I'm talking about. They have been in the trenches, they have the battle scars and they, like me, try not to take it all too seriously.

Don't get me wrong, we take the work itself very seriously. We are dealing with multimillion-pound projects, and the changes we make, if they go wrong, could cost our companies millions, and frequently affect people's lives and jobs. But being able to laugh at ourselves and see the funny side of things helps to alleviate some of the stress.

I continued to post on LinkedIn, and suggestions began to pop up that I should write a book based on the theme of my posts. I decided to test the level of interest, and that's how the name of the book came about. I did a quick test poll before launching myself headfirst into the world of publishing. There were two options...'Yes, can't wait to read it', or 'No, I would rather eat a cactus'.

And a whole 96% of respondents said, 'Yes, do it!' And so here we are! You're all caught up.

Let's get into it and find out how projects get started.

Acknowledgement

There are many people to thank, without whom this book would not exist. The first of those is my beloved coach Ann Stevenson, who has, over many years, given me the confidence and self-belief to be me, to do my own thing, and to find my voice. If you want to do big things, Ann is your woman. Secondly, I want to acknowledge Natasha Cleeve, top-notch recruitment consultant and all-around good egg, for starting the LinkedIn thread that ended up with the idea that we have a book in the first place. Here we are, it's all your fault, Natasha!

Deborah Hicks, Technical Consultant on all things project-related, Bella Osbourne and Anke Herrmann for expert insight into book writing and publishing. Thank you, you are all very inspiring women.

The members of the Secret Cactus Club Group: Swetta Coopamah, Sarah Anderson, Habib Butt, Natasha Pye, Christopher Rose, Steve Wakefield, Fiona Irvine, Helen Lomas, Helen Goddard and, our resident Agile expert, Dr. Derrick Gray. Your support, encouragement, and insights into all things project-related kept me on my toes, and kep me motivated. Thank you!

Shannon Cave did a marvellous job of editing the book, and making suggestions for improvements. She also dealt admirably with my erratic use of the comma and aversion to consistency in *italicising* words. Thank you Shannon. You are a star. And very patient.

And lastly, my lovely husband, Roque. Rock by name, rock by nature. Thank you for always supporting me in everything, however crazy. Forever and ever.

1

Project Initiation

What Is a Project?

Most standard project textbooks will give you a lengthy description of what is and what isn't a project. However, all you need
to know at this stage is this:

*A project is a temporary piece of work to achieve a specific outcome
or goal with a defined end date.*

It needs money, people, and an agreed-upon scope. And then
we are off. We have a project!

Simple, yes? Well...let's begin by demystifying some of those
terms!

In projects, we refer to the 'money' to run the project as the
project budget, and we show how we plan to spend it in a *cost
plan*. The 'people' element includes those working on the actual

project, the project team, and also includes other *stakeholders* who are impacted by the change in some way. The 'scope' refers to what is included in the project, and should also clarify what will *not* be included in the project. We'll go into each of these in more detail as we move on.

We should also be clear that a project is not a programme, and that it differs from process improvement work.

Eh, what?

There is often confusion about the difference between a project, a programme, and process improvement. Let's also look at each before we move on.

A programme can be a group of projects which will achieve a specific goal, e.g. a business transformation programme could include three individual projects—moving to a new location, changing the structure of the business, and creating a new online system for customers. Delivering all of these projects combined will achieve the overall programme goal of transforming the business.

A programme can also relate to an ongoing programme of work that will never end. For example, a bank may have a Regulatory Change programme. Every new project established to address a new piece of regulation will be a part of that programme.

Process improvement is not really a project as such. It's a discipline in its own right that looks at the operational processes in a business area, e.g. in Customer Service or a function such as Human Resources (HR). The intention is to look at ways of removing inefficiencies from the processes, eliminating issues that regularly cause process fails, or finding ways to automate parts of a process. And, just to confuse things, process improvement work can become a project.

For example, there may be a need to review the processes for issuing monthly bank statements to customers. There are many processes involved, as well as many different departments. The work to review these processes may be pulled together into the Statements Review Project. A Project Manager would be appointed to oversee the project, but the work would be carried out by Process Improvement Specialists.

And finally, you will frequently hear people referring to the project management methodology they use, which is typically either the *waterfall approach* or the *Agile approach*.

Waterfall means that the project will follow a sequential flow of five key phases, often referred to as the *project lifecycle*:

Initiation, Planning, Execution, Testing, and Closure

For the purposes of this book, we will focus on the waterfall approach.

The Agile methodology takes a different, more iterative, approach, and we will look at that in more detail in Chapter 11.

Now that we have all of that sorted, let's explore how businesses decide which projects to do.

This is where things start to get a little bit more complicated. Many projects need a lot of money, or *budget*. And some need a lot of people. Who also cost money. And most organisations are not too happy to spend money or release people from their day jobs to work on a project unless they have some guarantee that they're going to get a worthwhile return for their investment. And assurances that the project team won't mess up. And make things worse than they were before.

The organisation must, therefore, have a process to ensure it's spending money on doing the right things. People come up with great ideas all the time, but there has to be a way of sorting the wheat from the chaff. Which ones will deliver the most benefit for the organisation?

This is referred to as *idea generation* and takes place in what we call the *initiation* phase of the project. Different organisations will do this in different ways, but it will more than likely follow a similar approach to the one outlined below. The most important thing is to ensure that it's done in a structured way!

The structure applied to the process is known as the *governance process*.

What? We're not running a country; we just want to start a project!

Let me explain...

The Project Governance Process

Most organisations will have a process in place for deciding which projects they want to fund in the coming year. However, I have worked in some organisations where the process either wasn't very well known, or wasn't used properly, or wasn't fit for purpose!

But, in most cases, there's a governance process to follow, and you need to find out who 'owns' it.

Often, it's the Project Office Manager (POM) or the Head of Change/Projects. Whoever it is in your organisation, find out, and make them your new best friend! If you ask them nicely, they will talk you through the process and tell you what you need to do next.

The governance process outlines the key steps to get a project from idea to completion. We will look at each of these stages as we go through the book, but let's start with an *idea*.

Ideas

You've had a brilliant idea! It will make millions for the business. You just need to convince your boss and get it approved and boom! It's straight up to the top floor with a lovely brass nameplate on your new office door.

Whoa there! Slow down a bit! I don't want to dampen your enthusiasm, but the reality is that 95% of project ideas never get past the first hurdle. There are so many things that need to be considered before you even get a chance to present your case. And many hoops to be jumped through.

Let's have a look at some of the hoops.

The Ideas Funnel

This is the first stage for getting a project approved, or *initiated*. Ideas are generally collated across the organisation into a central point. This is usually the Project Management Office (PMO), or it could sit with the Finance function, or with someone in the leadership team, or an executive, such as the Chief Operating Officer (COO).

Their job is to help the senior management team decide which are the best projects to invest in for the future of the business.

The ideas are initially scored against specific criteria. Some of the most frequently used criteria include:

Strategic Fit – Is this idea actually aligned to where we are going as a business? Will it help us meet our goals? Will it add value to the share price (will people place more value on our company because we are going to be more profitable?)? Will it help our customers? Will it make us more efficient?

Most companies will set out a five-year *strategic plan* for their business. This explains what they want to achieve in terms of growing the business, entering new markets (finding new customers in different locations or by introducing new products), becoming more profitable/more efficient, or bringing new innovations to market.

The *project portfolio* should contain discretionary projects that will support the business strategy.

Return on Investment - Is it something that's worth spending money on because it will generate more money for the business?

At this stage, it's very difficult to quantify this, because you don't know how much the project is going to cost. And the potential benefits can only be estimated. But most people will hazard a guess to help their project get to the next stage! We will look more at this when we discuss *business case* and *cost-benefit analysis.*

Regulatory/Mandatory Changes – The project request should contain details about why the change is necessary, including information on any regulations that need to be complied with or any equipment or software that needs to be replaced.

Risk Assessment – If we make the change, what could go wrong? And if we *don't* do it, what could go wrong?

A risk is something that could happen in the future that would have a negative impact on the business. The project request form may ask for the risk to be quantified in monetary terms and the probability of it actually happening. This is a *tangible risk*, something that can be easily quantified.

For example, if we do a project to update the cash machine network of the bank and it goes wrong, our customers won't be able to use our cash machines. This could be assessed as having a 50% probability of happening, at a cost of £1m per day (lost revenue or additional costs) for two days (the time it could take to fix it).

Similarly, we need to look at the risk of *not* doing something, e.g. not complying with regulation. The risk might be a fine from the regulator (quantifiable/tangible), as well as the *intangible risk* of bad publicity for the bank. Intangible risks are those that are harder to quantify.

For example, if a bank was found to be charging a higher rate than permitted for its overdraft facility and was fined by the regulator, this could deter people from opening an account with the bank. But how many people exactly? That's very difficult to quantify. We will look more at risk later and explain how to determine a value for this.

Pet Projects – The other criteria, and this is an unofficial one that you won't find documented anywhere, is the 'pet project'. It falls into the category of 'can you just do this project because I said so, despite the fact that it doesn't score highly against any of the criteria, and may cost a fortune to deliver, but I want it anyway because I am really important and have great ideas' project request from senior management.

It's very difficult to turn down the pet project. Even if the decisions are made by a panel rather than an individual, if the requestor wields sufficient power or influence within the organisation, it's unlikely that anyone will stand up to them and point out the inadequacies of their proposal.

In this situation, the only sensible approach is to overwhelm them with helpful facts!

What do I mean by this? Isn't that a lot of wasted effort?

Trust me, it's better to spend time now creating a mini-*business case* (we'll come to this shortly), which shows very clearly the vast amount of resources and people that would be required to complete the project, than to waste six months and lots of valuable project budget because it went ahead and then failed.

If the proposer still insists on proceeding, then your business case didn't contain enough people required from their area and from their department budget to ensure a successful delivery.

And if that approach fails, then there is always a risk or compliance issue that can derail the dodgiest of project proposals before they get moving. You just need to look for them! Look harder!

Now that the project request form has been completed, the idea has been submitted to the project office, and assessed by the PMO Manager or Head of Change. Feedback has been received, and you've made the changes and obtained the additional information requested.

We can start the project now, right? Sorry! Not yet. Another activity for the PMO Manager is to assess all of the submitted ideas and create a report for the Project Investment Board (PIB). They decide which projects go forward and which get put on the back burner or dropped completely.

The report provides an assessment of the number of projects requested, the total potential spend if all of the projects were approved, and, most importantly, an assessment of 'doability'.

Doah what now?

Doability. This means several things in project world. Let me explain...

In the simplest scenario, it means can the organisation physically deliver all of the requested changes? Do they have enough Project Managers, for example? It also means, can the organisation support all of the changes made in the proposed timescales? If every project on a list of twenty projects needs four people from the Operations team to help deliver all of the projects within six months, and the Operations team only has sixty people on it, then 'Houston, we have a problem'!

Then there is *change fatigue*. What? How can we be tired? We haven't started the project yet?

I know, but bear with me. For the people on the receiving end of all the changes happening in the organisation, it can get a bit overwhelming. If you think again about the Operations team, working in a customer service centre or call centre for example, in an organisation that has three big projects all landing at the same time, it could get very confusing.

They may use three different systems to do their jobs, and if each one is changing at the same time, with an impact on procedures and processes, they are going to get annoyed pretty quickly. And more so if any of the changes creates uncertainty about their jobs.

Organisations keep track of this by creating a *roadmap* or *landing schedule* for the organisation. This is a calendar view of all of the changes across all areas of the business. It may also show whether the impact is minor or significant, or just for information.

I like to do one using large sheets of flipchart paper taped together with a pictorial view of what changes are landing when into each department. It's a great visual aid to planning change in a large organisation, as it's easy to see at a glance if any area is going to be overloaded at any one time. However, there are loads of applications that allow you to do this online as well if you are working with a virtual team. Just have a look for 'virtual whiteboard application'.

We also need to think about technical feasibility and risk. Is it practical to change several major systems at the same time? If something goes wrong with one of them, could it impact any other systems, even bringing the organisation to a halt?

To manage this, most organisations will have a r*elease schedule* or r*elease management approach*. This is similar to the landing schedule, but it is IT-focused, and is usually managed within the IT Department.

This schedule contains all of the changes impacting the organisation's IT systems. Not just from projects, but the routine maintenance, system and security upgrades, and other housekeeping activities that they undertake on a regular basis.

Having this view allows the IT Managers to ensure that a new system implementation won't clash with a large maintenance upgrade.

Change fatigue and technical feasibility alone are not necessarily reasons for discounting an idea, but they will be a consideration in terms of the timing of doing them. The leadership team may decide that there are just too many big ideas in play at this stage and agree to delay some of them for consideration in later years.

This initial filtering of ideas through the first stage of the funnel will narrow down the options to hopefully less than twenty viable ideas. More than that and the process becomes unmanageable.

This initial shortlist of ideas can then be shared with the Project Investment Board (PIB) in more detail.

The Project Investment Board

The PIB is a meeting of senior managers representing different areas of the business who make decisions on which projects should proceed to the next stage. They will look at the viability of each proposal and whether it fits with the business strategy.

Often, the project proposer or their deputy is asked to talk through the project idea, but, generally, it will be a presentation outlining the purpose of the project, what outcomes and benefits it's expected to achieve, some high-level costs, and a timeline. It may also be scored against the selection criteria described above.

At this stage, there is no need to go into detail about the proposed solution. The paper should concentrate on what problem needs to be solved and the benefits to the business of solving that problem.

Once the idea is presented, it then becomes a little bit like a beauty pageant...the various sponsors/presenters will promote their ideas and encourage other members of the PIB to approve them. In some organisations, a further scoring or voting system will be applied during the meeting to narrow down the list if there are too many projects proposed. Good governance dictates that everyone should vote for the projects that most benefit the company. However, many managers will vote for the project that brings most benefit to *their* area of the business. And, in some cases, those who wield the most power or influence in the group will influence others to vote for *their* project.

And this is how projects that should never have seen the light of day get through to the next stage! Especially the pet projects!

Ideas may be approved to move onto the next stage, the business case, or they may be given partial or seed funding to explore the idea in more detail and revert with more robust cost and benefit forecasts. This may involve the creation of a pilot or *proof of concept* (POC) mini-project to prove that the idea has merit. A POC may involve creating and implementing the solution in one location only, or trialling a new application for a specific set of customers or employers, for example.

Project selection is the first step in delivering successful projects. If businesses don't base their project selection decisions on a robust process aligned to achieving their strategic goals, things can start to go wrong:

1. They will deliver a high-profile and exciting, brilliantly executed project that delivers absolutely nothing of value to the organisation (typically this would be a pet project!).

or

2. The essential project that was crucial to the success of the business either isn't done or fails because it is underfunded or under-resourced, or under-supported by senior management, because the big, exciting project was prioritised instead.

or

3. In the worst-case scenario, a project isn't fully understood at the outset and doesn't score highly enough in any of the criteria. It isn't approved, or is delayed, and the organisation suffers a significant loss as a result.

This latter scenario often occurs with respect to regulatory projects. You would think large organisations would have learned their lessons by now. But they haven't. Take the implementation of the Basel II regulations in the UK banking sector in the mid-2000s, for example. This was a regulatory project that was supposed to help banks manage their financial position and understand the risk in their operations. Great focus was placed on creating new systems and implementing hugely complicated calculations to forecast potential disasters and the potential impact these would have on loan portfolios. But, by 2008, many of the banks had gone bust, were taken over, or needed government support to continue.

Why? Because the project wasn't just about changing the systems and making great calculations. These banks failed because of the behaviour of the people working in them. The project had been misunderstood at the outset and had focused on changing the technical aspects of the business, and not the organisation's culture.

This, didn't just cost the banks themselves millions of £s, it also cost people their homes, businesses, jobs, and future pensions.

On that unhappy note, let's make sure we think very carefully about all aspects of change and how we apply our selection criteria, before we approve or dismiss any project proposals.

With large projects, and even larger budgets, comes great responsibility!

Chapter 1 Summary - What Have We Learned?

- What makes a project, and the difference between a project, a programme, and process improvement
- The stages of the project lifecycle
- The governance process
- Idea generation and the ideas funnel
- The role of the Project Investment Board

2

The Business Case & Project Charter

The PIB has approved the idea to move to the next stage, to conduct further investigation. A Project Manager (PM) has been appointed to find out in more detail if there is merit in investing money in the idea and will present the findings back to the PIB in the form of a business case. Ideally, the business case should be prepared by someone external to the Project Team, such as the Business Department head that will benefit most from its implementation. But this rarely happens, and, generally, the PM will draft the document, obtaining input from the business and sponsor, before obtaining their approval to submit the final version to the PIB.

The Business Case

The business case (which can also be called a Project Initiation Document or PID) gives a high-level overview of the proposed approach to the project, outlining estimated costs and the potential benefits. It may propose alternative approaches with a cost-benefit analysis1 for each one, the anticipated benefits, and the cost for each approach.

A *feasibility study* may also be required. Whereas the business case looks at whether the project is worth doing from a benefits perspective, the feasibility study is concerned with whether the organisation can carry it out successfully.

The feasibility study will assess:

- The technical feasibility of the project: Is the proposed solution a reasonable approach to the problem it's trying to fix? Does the organisation have the technical capability, capacity, information, and facilities to deliver the project?
- The financial feasibility: Does the organisation have the funds to complete the work?
- The legal feasibility: Are there any legal requirements that may constrain the project?
- The operational feasibility: Will the project outcomes address the organisation's operational needs?
- The scheduling feasibility: Can the work be completed in the time available, and is there enough resource capacity available?

The cost-benefit analysis information will provide input to the financial aspect of the feasibility study, as well as give an indication of resource requirements, as the business case also shows the resources required for each option. This includes people working on the project, people supporting the project (e.g., SMEs from the operational areas), and any additional resources (such as extra office space).

18

A more detailed risk assessment is included in the business case, showing the outcome if the project does not go ahead, and the potential risks if it does go ahead, for each of the proposed solutions. This is done in more detail than the project request form and should contain more accurate probability and impact costs. It should also contain information on any *dependencies*, those things that need to happen for the project to be successful (such as the provision of SMEs from the Operations team). Any assumptions are also added to ensure that something important isn't forgotten. For example, it is assumed that there will be funding available to complete the project.

The PM will work with an *Architect* to determine the best approach to take for the project from an IT perspective. The Architect understands all of the systems in the business, how they fit together, and how data moves between the systems. He or she will also know if there is a solution in place already that could be adapted to solve the problem without spending too much money.

The business case should also contain a list of individual roles or departments, or other stakeholders, such as customers, who will be impacted by the changes. They may need to approve the business case or provide input before it can be presented back to the PIB.

Once completed and approved by the Project Sponsor, the business case is submitted to the PIB. The Project Sponsor's approval of the business case is crucial, because they will be held responsible for ensuring the project benefits are actually delivered. Expect them to be very interested in how the costs and benefits were calculated and to play an active part in ensuring the success of the project.

Their name is going on it, and the 'benefits' to the business may mean that their budget will be cut next year. They will want to make sure the benefits are not overstated and that the project has a high probability of being successful. And, apart from anything else, no one wants to be associated with a failed project!

If it's approved by the PIB, the project will be allocated a project budget and a cost centre code from the Finance team. This ensures that any money spent on the project can be tracked to ensure it doesn't go over budget. Sometimes the PIB will only release part of the budget to complete part of the work and ask the project team to return once they have completed it to request the remainder of the budget.

If you have a Finance team that can organise this without you promising to name your first-born child after the Finance Manager, then you are destined for success!

To be fair to Finance, it's usually not their fault. They have inherited an accounts management system that isn't particularly project-friendly, or was possibly set up by goatherds. Who were busy trying to knit socks at the same time. Your friendly Finance business partner will spend much time explaining to you about cost-centres and WBS (work breakdown structure) codes and how it's all going to take place in the monthly cycle.

Just nod along and ask them to email you when it's done. Or you risk wasting years of your life trying to understand it. Which is pointless. Because it cannot be understood by anyone who is not an accountant. Or a goatherd. We must focus on delivering the project and hope that Finance is able to get it together before the project is closed (which doesn't always happen).

The Project Charter

Information from the business case and the PIB decision is transferred into a document called the Project Charter. This document authorises the existence of a project and confirms the purpose of it and how it should be delivered. It will contain at a minimum:

- Project purpose and *key deliverables* – usually five or six goals or objectives that the project should fulfill
- *Success criteria* for each deliverable
- *High-level business requirements* – such as, 'the new system must do this...'
- Any *constraints, dependencies, assumptions, risks* or current *issues*
- Some *high-level milestones*
- Approved *budget* and *resources*
- The *key stakeholder* list
- *Success criteria* for the project (so that we know the project is complete)
- The approval process to say the project is complete, and who signs it off
- The Project Manager and Project Sponsor names with their level of *delegated authority,* the level of spend they can

approve on the project

The Project Charter will be presented to the PIB or PMO for approval in a process known as the *stage gate* process. It is checked to make sure all of the previously stated criteria have been met, e.g. any project Key Performance Indicators or other PMO criteria.

Once approved, the project can move on to the next stage, and the Project Charter document essentially forms the basis of the agreement between the PIB and the project team. When issues arise later, or there is a dispute or a decision that needs to be made, it can be referred back to. The document should be signed off by the Project Sponsor at a minimum. Some organisations require the charter to be signed off by the PIB and/or members of the executive or management team, especially if they have committed resources to work on the project. If this is the case, always make sure this is written down, preferably in blood! Once everyone has agreed it, the contents of the Charter shouldn't be changed without the authorisation of the original approver(s).

Don't worry if you don't understand all of the terms in the Project Charter just yet. We will cover them in more detail in the next chapter.

Yay! Finally, we are ready to start the project!

Chapter 2 Summary - What Have We Learned?

- The information required in the business case
- Why a cost-benefit analysis is required
- What a feasibility study is and what it involves
- The purpose of the Project Charter and what is included in it

3

Kicking Off the Project

We've got the green light, and we are ready to go! Let's get this party started! Oh, wait, hang on, we don't have anyone to party with...yet! Let's take a look at that.

Resourcing the Project & Assembling the Team

The first thing we need to do is set up the project team. We already know which resources (people/roles) have been approved because they were in the business case. Now we need to contact the department heads to agree who will fill each role. If there is an established project or change function in the business, and a Head of Change, this might be something they discuss at a weekly managers' meeting. Or it may be something that's discussed at the PIB.

Do not be surprised if the department head claims to have no knowledge of this resource request, or its approval at the PIB, of which they were a part. They will develop a sudden case of amnesia at any request to provide people from their team to support a project. Unless it is doing something for their department. In which case they will grudgingly give you a name in exchange for a promise that you will return the person within the agreed-upon period, unscathed by the experience.

Agree to the former (you both know you are lying), and pretend you didn't hear the latter as you wander off, mumbling about owing them a coffee.

The main challenge is ensuring the resource will be made available. Congratulations if you have secured this. It is a battle of wits, but rest assured that Project Managers always win. Because it's written down and approved in the business case, and so it must be true.

But be aware that there is also the bunfight for the 'best' resource.

As an example, in a project to move customer service activities to a new system, the PM is going to want a Subject Matter Expert (SME) who is highly experienced in the old system, rather than someone who has just joined the team fairly recently.

You might think this is strange. Why do they want someone who knows the *old* system when it's being replaced?

Because an important rule of project world is ensuring we document the current state, the 'as is' before we go on to document what we want from the new system, the 'to be' state. We will look at this in more detail when we come to talk about *business requirements,* but, essentially, we need to know what the systems do currently, and what processes are in place, so that we don't forget to add some essential step or requirement to the new system.

There may also be competition among Project Managers to get resources they have worked with before on a similar project. There may also be some colleagues that they *don't* want to work with, perhaps if they didn't produce the work on time on a previous project. This can often result in a bit of horse trading among the project community to ensure they get the experience and knowledge they need on their projects.

The Kick-off Workshop

Once each of the project roles has been filled, the Project Manager will usually organise what's known as a *kick-off workshop.* Don't worry, nobody gets kicked-off the project team! We need all the help we can get!

This is where the new team comes together, perhaps meeting each other for the first time, and finding out a bit more about the project.

A good Project Manager will issue an agenda before the meeting, and will perhaps include the business case, to give the team members some background information about the project.

Here's an example agenda:

AGENDA

1. Introductions & Icebreaker Exercise
2. Roles & Responsibilities
3. High-level Plan Walkthrough
4. Risks, Assumptions, Issues, Dependencies
5. Future Meetings & Ways of Working
6. Actions

Before the meeting begins, the Project Manager may suggest an ice-breaker exercise to help the team get to know each other a little better. Depending on the group dynamic, these can be excruciatingly awkward, or good fun and serve their purpose. I once worked for someone who thought it was a good idea to put on a Velcro® jester's hat and have the team throw fuzzy balls at his head*. I have no words. May none of your ice-breaker exercises ever involve dressing up...or throwing things.

Once the fun/awkward activities are out of the way, the first topic of the meeting should be an overview of what the project is about, what the goals are, and then an opportunity to ask questions. This latter part needs to be managed carefully, as it can run on. Everyone generally has a lot of questions, most of which can't be answered at this stage!

Next is the Project Manager's chance to explain what is required from each person on the project team. Any assumptions need to be stated and confirmed to avoid the 'oh, I thought you were doing that' scenario from arising later!

The easiest way to do this is to create a *Responsibility Assignment Matrix* (RAM) showing who is Responsible (R) for performing the key tasks, who Approves (A) it when it's finished, and who is a Contributor to its completion (C).

The RAM should include every member of the project team and all of the key deliverables. That's all that's needed at the moment. As the project plan is developed, these key deliverables will be broken down into *milestones* and tasks with the name of the person responsible for delivering it attached to each task in the plan.

Deliverable	Project Sponsor	Project Manager	Business Analyst	SME Ops	Lead Developer
Project Plan	A	R	C	C	C
Design	A	A	C	C	R
Business Requirements	A	A	R	C	-

Example – Responsibility Matrix

Project Managers may have their own version of the RAM, and it may depend on what is used or recommended by your organisation's project office. You may also come across a RACI matrix (Responsible, Accountable, Consult, Inform), but I use that for a different purpose. Remember how the RAM was used to talk about tasks? I use the RACI to show what's required for stakeholders. We will go into this in more detail when we talk about *stakeholder engagement.*

The key deliverables will now have been allocated across the project team. However, there may still be some responsibilities that need to be clarified. And there may also be some people in the project team who aren't 'project people' and don't really understand what's going on and what you need from them.

To avoid confusion, I produce an outline for each role in the team with what I expect them to do. Once agreed upon with the team member, I put these into the Project Management Plan (PMP) document. I always talk it through with each member of the team to make sure they really understand what each task or responsibility is and, more importantly, how they are going to do it. Very often, people don't want to admit that they don't know how to do something they think they should know how to do (one of the reasons for this book!), and it's better to talk them through your thinking than find out the night before a deadline that they haven't started!

Your organisation will likely have its own formal outline of project responsibilities, but there's a brief overview of the main roles in a project team in Chapter 4.

Back to the kick-off workshop. The next thing is a walkthrough of the high-level plan. At this stage, the Project Manager and Architect may have an idea of how the project will be delivered, but this needs to be confirmed in a *planning workshop*. We will cover that shortly, but, for now, it's enough that the team has an idea of the project timescale.

Based on the discussion around the timeline, the team may begin to call out risks (things that may go wrong in the future) and issues (things that already exist that could prevent the project from moving forward). These will be captured to add to the RAID (Risks, Assumptions, Issues, Dependencies) log (we will get to that in more detail when we cover the contents of the PMP below).

Finally, the Project Manager should talk about how the team will work together going forward. A meeting schedule may be proposed, or they may have already developed the full governance structure of the project (see the PMP section on project governance below).

Either way, the team shouldn't leave the meeting until they know when they are next getting together and have agreed on the timescale for completing any actions from the meeting.

And now our project has officially begun!

Let's move on to the next chapter and take a look at who does what in project world.

*No one was hurt in the kicking-off of that project...unfortunat ely.

Chapter 3 Summary - What Have We Learned?

- · How to get the project team assembled
- · What a kick-off workshop is and what's involved in running one
- · A process for assigning responsibilities to the project team

4

Project Roles

In this chapter we will have a look at who does what on the project team. If you are reading this and you work in HR (Human Resources) please forgive my slightly tongue-in-cheek guide to the key roles on a project team. In my defence, it's all true!

Key Project Roles

1. The Project Sponsor

The head honcho, the key decision-maker, the boss, God... In terms of the hierarchy in a project team the sponsor is the main man/woman.

Ah yes, the lesser spotted but highly elusive Project Sponsor.

Every project must have one, but, sometimes, after project approval, they can be hard to track down!

So how does one catch a Project Sponsor?

Sometimes it's easy. Sponsors are generally members of the executive/leadership team. The people who hold the purse strings. In most companies, unless there is a central project pot, project funding will come out of their budget.

They will come up with a fabulous idea for a project and will approach the Head of Change/PMO Manager for support in getting it through the project approval process.

However, often someone in IT, or an area with insufficient budget for projects, will come up with a fabulous/essential project idea and have to scurry around trying to find someone to sponsor it.

Once onboard, the sponsor will submit the project for approval and chair project board meetings.

The best sponsors are those who are engaged, understand the purpose of the project, and who provide leadership and support to the project team. And make decisions.

If you can catch them!

If you have ever tried to get in the diary of an executive manager, you will know that this is a difficult thing indeed. It takes cunning and influencing skills to be able to get past their assistants and nab a space in their diary.

Never arrange to meet them anywhere else other than their

office. This is a rookie mistake. Standing outside their office means you can guard the door to ensure they don't slip away. They may try to push past you mumbling something about toilets or coffee. Do not let them out of your sight!

But be nice to your sponsor. They usually pay for the end of project party.

2. The Project Manager

We have talked a lot about what Project Managers do already, but, essentially, they are responsible for figuring out how to get the project moving. Which is sometimes akin to pushing a large boulder up a hill. While other people stand around and talk about how big the boulder is. And how great it will be when it gets to the top of the hill. Or how much money having the boulder in a different place will save them. The poor PM must focus on the boulder and push it around all of the people who are now standing in the way.

The PM is responsible for coordinating the writing of the business case. They can't do it alone, they need input from others, e.g. Finance, the Sponsor, and the Business Analyst. The purpose of the business case is to obtain funding approval, and the PM will spend a lot of time coordinating the BAs and SMEs to gather requirements, working with them, and the Architect, to develop the project plan and approach.

Once the project is underway, the Project Manager keeps people informed, especially the Sponsor and project team, chairs project meetings, sees problems coming on the horizon, and puts actions in place to avoid them. They spend a lot of time solving disagreements between BAs and SMEs (mostly), translate IT speak for the Sponsor and business heads, and tell users what's coming and what they need to do to be ready. They also get to explain why the project isn't on track or is over budget at project board meetings. Which is always fun! In the same way that interrogation under a very bright spotlight is fun.

A good Project Manager knows a little about a lot of things, and use this knowledge to solve problems. They are excellent negotiators and influencers, because goddammit, they are very, very determined that their project will deliver on time. And within budget. Even although they know that this very rarely happens.

Which means they usually drink wine of an evening.

3. The IT Architect

The Yodas of project world.

The Architect is the first port of call when someone comes up with a brilliant project idea. They are very experienced IT people with a broad knowledge of lots of different systems/applications.

They will likely tell you that what you want already exists, it just hasn't been switched on yet. Or that someone has already tried to do this a few years ago. And failed because there was no 'appetite' for it.

But they are generally very helpful, and passionate about what they do, and will try to find you a solution. In a calm and nurturing way.

If it's something new that requires any IT work, they give a view of the best way to approach the project and know what systems will likely be impacted. And roughly how long it will take to investigate the approach. This is essential for your budget and resource estimates.

Architects are generally very sensible people, who can give an objective view of why a senior manager's 'pet project' isn't the best allocation of scarce project funds. Which is super helpful when difficult conversations need to take place! Make sure they are on your Project Investment Board (where decisions are made on which projects get funded) and that you have an agreed view and approach before meeting! They can help to provide support and explain the complicated reasons why the 'pet project' isn't possible.

If you are a Project Manager, make friends with the IT Architect.

4. The Business Analyst

The Business Analyst (BA) is the unsung hero of the project world. If you don't have one on your project, there's a good chance your project will fail.

Why?

Because they build the foundations of a successful project. I guess, they could be called the bricklayers of project world! And the very senior and experienced ones, called Business Architects, are the master builders, passing on their knowledge and wisdom to the younger generation.

Their first job is to define the scope of the project. Without a clear scope, there's a risk that your project will wander all over the place and not deliver.

They map out the 'As Is' and 'To Be' process(es) that will change. When time is short, it's tempting to skip the 'As Is' bit and go straight to the solution—don't do this! Because this is where mistakes happen!

When people are immersed in a business process, doing it daily, they forget about the workarounds that they carry out without thinking. But that workaround masks a key step in the process. And unless a BA is on the ball, monitoring every step as they walk through the process, then it will get missed.

And when someone says later 'oh, I didn't realise you needed that...', when it's too late to do anything about it, everyone will feel bad and wish they had completed the 'As Is' requirements. They may even feel so bad that they need to go off to the pub for a few beers. BAs often do this.

The next key step for the BA is to use the information they have gathered to define high-level requirements—what needs to change. This is called a *gap analysis* and forms the bones of the business case, cost estimates, scope, and then the *Business Requirements Document.*

Once these documents are approved, the BA can begin providing input to the training and communications materials, while continuing to make updates to the new processes as the project moves through development and testing.

When it's all over, and it's project party time, the BAs are the ones who drink beer, get a bit rowdy, then start dancing—they don't get out often. Well, except the occasional trip to the pub—see above.

5. The PMO Manager

The PMO Managers are the elephants of project world.

Any good Head of Projects will tell you that they cannot do their role properly without an effective Project Management Office Manager.

Because they remember every project decision ever made and can account for every penny of project spend, on every project, even when the Project Manager cannot.

They're responsible for ensuring that there is an effective methodology (guidelines) in place for managing projects. This is essential to ensure that projects are approved, managed, and reported in a consistent way. Allowing senior managers to compare how well their investments are doing by creating a level playing field.

PMO Managers provide an overall project portfolio status and quality report and sometimes the overall road map for the organisation to show what changes will land when, and for whom.

They also control the Project Investment Board and *stage gate process*. PMs must demonstrate that they have met specific criteria before their project may progress to the next stage, and obtain the next tranche of funding.

The PMO Manager cannot be bribed with wine, chocolate, or free coffee in relation to stage gates. So I hear...

6. The PMO Analyst

The Project Management Office Analyst role is one of the most misunderstood and underutilised in the project world.

Firstly, they are not admin assistants! They are often asked to take meeting notes, collate status reports, and produce reporting packs, and that's all fine, as it can free up some of the PM's time. But it's really a waste of their talents and doesn't add any real value to the project.

What they should be doing is *analysing* project information. The clue is in the job title!

Which means?

Working closely with Project Managers to understand the project, the project plan, and the RAID log. They can then analyse the status reports and identify gaps, highlight missing risks and dependencies, and ensure that projects are on track. There are numerous measures that can be examined to confirm the real status of the project, and we will look at some of these later.

But isn't that analysis the job of the PM?

Yes and no. The PMO Analyst can add value by doing the initial analysis and sharing it with the PM, who can then act on it.

The PMO Analyst can also take a forward-looking role, focusing on forecasting upcoming milestones and the probability of achieving them, expected monthly costs, any benefits due, and any risks and issues that need to be addressed.

Why is this more useful than reporting what happened last month?

Because a forward-looking report gives the Project Manager and business leaders things that they can act on. Even the best leaders cannot change the past!

PMO Analysts often progress to become excellent PMO Managers or Project Managers. It makes sense to give them a great learning experience by getting them properly involved in projects, and not simply as glorified admin assistants!

They also bring cake to work. They are the reason you can't shift that last five pounds.

7. The Business Readiness Manager

The Business Readiness Manager (BRM) may also be known as the Business Mobilisation Manager (BMM). They are the ones who get the business ready and excited for the changes. The project party people, if you like.

Their job is making sure that the project lands well with users and customers.

This role is often seen as a luxury, something that the PM should do. But, on a large project, with lots of users, it's not possible for the PM to do it all.

The BRM ensures the business is ready for the change—again, the clue is in the job title!

But what does that actually mean? It means that they are responsible for making sure that communications and training are in place and distributed at the appropriate times. The BRM may not necessarily write the communications—that may be done by an in-house Communications Manager for example, or by the PM or Project Sponsor. But they are responsible for identifying who needs to be communicated with and what they need to hear.

The BRM will share issues and information on what's going

well or not so well. They provide feedback to the project team, acting as an almost independent conduit between them and the users/stakeholders.

They also work with the Test Manager to resource and coordinate UAT (*User Acceptance Testing*—where users try out a new system and report back). They work with business heads to agree on Key Performance Indicators (KPIs) for a new system and the acceptance criteria for the system to pass through testing to go live.

They may run workshops with BAs and SMEs from the business and run training/comms sessions.

They always have chocolate on their desks and are usually cheerful souls. Maybe because of the chocolate.

8. The Subject Matter Expert

The people who know what's broken...and can make or break the project.

Every project needs Subject Matter Experts (SMEs). They are people from functional areas of the business such as Operations, Finance, and HR. They are not Small or Medium Enterprises!

If you are lucky, you will get one who's a real expert in the job and in the use of existing systems and processes.

But this causes a problem.

Because their Line Manager doesn't want to give them up for three (really six!) months.

The Line Manager will perhaps offer a newbie, or an underperformer. They don't want to lose the best people from their team, as this will cause them more issues.

But a good PM will already know who they want and will fight to the death to secure their SME of choice. Often this means the same SMEs being requested multiple times by different PMs.

Which gives rise to the common project management practice known as 'horse trading'. Where PMs trade favours to secure resources.

Once on a project, there is little chance of escape for the SME.

Their input is required to map current processes, define requirements for the new system/product, create test scripts, do testing and training, and deliver project-related communications to their business colleagues.

Many SMEs fall into the 'knowledge is power trap', enjoying the *Secret Squirrel* nature of their newfound status, and never want to go back to the day job.

But they can also morph into the role of *change champion*, promoting the change to their colleagues, sharing information, and building excitement about the launch. They must, therefore, be coddled and bought many coffees to ensure they don't disappear back into the business never to return.

9. The Test Manager (& Testers)

The time travellers of the project world...

Being a Test Manager is a bit of a thankless task. But it does give the opportunity for time travel. Nobody really understands what they do (unless they work in testing), and nobody really wants to know either. They just want to know that everything is okay with their new system or data migration, that it's all just peachy.

Well, that doesn't just happen. There is a lot of work that goes on behind the scenes to make sure that testing can actually take place. The first thing to understand is what kind of testing is required. We will look at testing in more detail in Chapter 8, but, generally, we need to know that the system works, it does what we expect, and that people know how to use it.

This first aspect is called *non-functional testing*, meaning that we switch it on and it works and it's fast enough, etc. Nobody wants to use a system that takes three days to load a page, or freezes when more than six people log into it.

The second is *functional testing*, which means that, when we put in information, we get the expected result or outcome. For example, if we wanted a system that showed all of the accounts a customer had, or everything they ever bought from our company, we would put in the client's account number and their information would show up. Without anything missing, or without adding in another customer's information.

Then we have User Acceptance Testing (UAT), which means that the users, in the service centre or call centre for example, can follow the process written by the Business Analysts, and the system takes them through it in the correct order, without stalling midway.

The Test Manager needs to know which tests are required for each project and makes sure that they have what's called a *test environment* to do the testing. It's very rare that an organisation would want to test anything in their live environment…the risk is too high that something will go wrong. And if it can go wrong, it surely will!

There is much competition for access to test environments, the replications of the real world system where testing is done. Test Managers have to be made of stern stuff to withstand the wheedling and whining that they will be subjected to by Project Managers looking for 'a test slot', which sounds like a dentist appointment, but can be a six- or eight-week window, locking out everyone else who also urgently needs access 'or their whole project will fail'.

They must juggle conflicting demands (I refer you to the release management approach mentioned previously, which doesn't always work well) and ensure they have sufficient testers to conduct all of the testing.

SMEs who have not been involved in the process before must be trained in writing the test scripts (what processes need to be tested) and then carry out the tests.

The *test window,* the time needed to complete the testing, is always underestimated in the planning stage. Then, as the project progresses and time starts to run out, the test window will be squeezed as it comes nearer the end of the project, when everyone else has 'had their chance to faff about with requirements gathering and development' (a direct quote from a Test Manager).

Unfortunately, they do not have the ability to go back in time and create more time to complete the testing. But they have mastered the ability to make time go faster and travel into the future!

How so?

The IT guys have cleverly invented an application which allows time-sensitive processes to be run faster. So that you don't have to spend a week observing a process which runs over seven days.

So, we're not going back to the future?

Not quite. But they can make things, like banking processes, appear as if they are running faster. Which, in some cases, is a miracle all of its own!

10. The Migration Manager

The Jedis of the project world...

Being a Migration Manager is a test of endurance and requires nerves of steel. The culmination of months of work and preparation generally comes down to one or two weekends of work where they have a chance to become rock stars, or damp squibs, in the matter of a few hours.

Whoa, that's a lot of pressure! What's all the fuss about?

The Migration Manager is responsible for the transition from the old system to the new system. Or for moving the data, e.g. customer and product information, from an old system to a new one.

Their main responsibility is to create a minute-by-minute (yes, it is *that* detailed) plan for the transition period.

Depending on the kind of project, there will usually be data to be uploaded, new systems to switch on, tests to be run to make sure it's all working, and, of course, some checks to be done on other systems to make sure something else hasn't been impacted by the implementation.

The migration will usually be completed by Sunday evening (if it's being done over the weekend), with everything back to normal and running smoothly by Monday morning. If this doesn't happen, the Migration Manager usually blames themself, which is unfair, as getting the project to this point is

47

always a team effort.

There are so many things that can go wrong that are out of the control of the Migration Manager. They often have to dust themselves off, focusing on the contingency plan and rectifying any issues. And then they get to go through the whole migration process again.

But, most of the time, it will all go swimmingly, and the team can enjoy a well-earned celebration.

These are the main roles in any project team. There may well be others in your organisation, but we have the basics and can now move on to the Project Management Plan!

Chapter 4 Summary - What Have We Learned?

· An understanding of the key roles in the project team

5

The Project Management Plan

Yes, another lengthy document talking about what we are going to do! I know you are all desperate to start *doing* something at this stage, but the most important part of project management is the planning!

When I first started out, one of the experienced Project Managers I worked with kept saying the same thing:

'If you fail to plan, you plan to fail.'

Now, after he said this for the tenth time, I actually wanted to hit him with one of his many weighty project folders (we were extremely paper-based at that point in time). However, I managed to restrain myself, only just, and recognised that he did have a point.

Planning is everything. Not only because it tells everyone what they need to do. And because it lets us figure out when we are likely to finish the work. And because it helps us figure out the stuff we hadn't thought of! It's also necessary, because it is really, really easy for the team to get absorbed in the details of the project, perhaps fixing a complex problem, and begin to lose their way. The PMP and its associated plans are what keep the team on track.

And once the project is approved, the easiest way to keep everyone on the same stage is to put all the plans and documents into one overall document, the Project Management Plan or PMP.

The PMP is a document, or collection of documents, that demonstrates how the project will be delivered. It shouldn't be confused with the actual project plan, which lists out the project tasks.

Apart from the role outlines we covered above, I also include the following in the PMP:

- The project governance process
- The project structure
- Project scope
- Milestones and project plans
- Resource plans
- Budget information and the cost plan
- Key Performance Indicators (KPIs) for the new system/process, e.g., how it's configured, how quickly things are done, service standards, etc.
- Key Success Criteria (KSCs) for the project (what we *must* deliver before the project can be signed off as complete)
- *Business readiness*, and communications and training plans

- The RAID (Risk, Assumptions, Issues and Dependencies) log
- Benefits and the benefits realisation plan

Let's look at each of these in more detail.

The Project Governance Process

Yes, more bureaucracy! But it's needed, honest! This is different from the overall project management governance process we covered earlier, as it deals specifically with this project. It outlines how the project will be managed and how decisions will be made. Pretty important when things get a bit tense and tempers are frayed!

The Project Structure

The size and complexity of the project, as well as the level of governance required, will dictate the structure of the project team. A small project team with a light-touch governance approach requires only a simple structure as in this example:

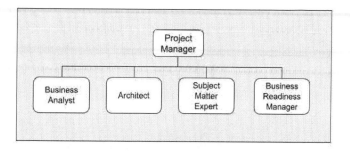

Example – Simple Project Structure

However, a larger team, with many members, or a programme, may need a more complex structure, as in Example 2, where workstream leads look after their own *workstream,* but report to the Project Manager.

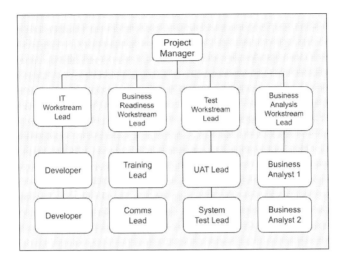

Example – Project Workstram Structure

A workstream is a way of breaking down the overall project into smaller, more manageable pieces of work, and we will look at that in more detail during the project plan section below.

The Project Board

The first element is the *project board* (sometimes called a project steering group or PSG). This is the decision-making body of the project and will usually meet on a monthly basis. The Project Sponsor chairs the meeting. As a minimum, the project board will usually include a representative from IT, someone from Finance, the Project Manager, and someone from the PMO. But I have been on boards where there were twenty members! Not the best for making decisons, or for getting through the agenda on time.

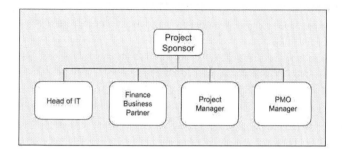

Example – A Project Board

The project board will review the current status report and look at any anomalies that require decisions. For example, a new risk may have been identified which requires immediate action to mitigate it. The Project Manager will make a recommendation, and the project board will make a decision. There will usually be other items on the agenda, including decisions that need to be made about the approach, approval of spending within the authority level of the board, and perhaps a discussion around the performance of any third-party suppliers.

The board will not be able to make all of its decisions in isolation. If the project is about to go over budget and additional funding is required, this would usually have to be approved by the PIB who initially approved the project. The project board can make the decision to request additional funding from the PIB, and the Project Manager can then complete a *change control* or *change request* document.

The change control is submitted to the PIB for approval, detailing why the additional funding is required. It should also be used to request an extension to the delivery date of the project and to change anything material in the scope.

What? Every decision needs to go to the PIB? Then what's the point in having the project board?

Well, this is the next part of the project governance process. The Project Manager will document the levels of *delegated authority* held by the project board. Which is basically a summary of what limits they have in making decisions related to the project.

The details of what the project board can authorise are captured in the PMP, along with the escalation route for any other decisions. In a large project, there has to be a way to resolve differences of opinion between project team members and between workstream leads. Not everything can be escalated to the Project Manager or Project Sponsor. Often, each workstream lead will have the authority to make their own decisions, but, again, limits will be set on this.

They may be permitted to agree to any expenditure increase up to £5000, for example, without having to revert to the PIB. Or to extend the timeline up to seven days.

Once the request goes over these limits, or cumulative requests breach these limits within a certain period, then they must be escalated to the PIB. The cumulative part is to prevent project boards from agreeing to extend their budget by £4999 three times, or to move the delivery deadline by six days three or four times!

Where agreement cannot be reached, let's say two workstream leads are arguing over who has priority for access to a test lab or to SME resources (this happens often), or a developer and Business Analyst disagree about the correct approach to the solution, then there is a documented escalation process to allow them to reach agreement.

Most Project Managers will tell you that they spend more time adjudicating between team members and resolving problems than anything else!

The Project Scope

The next thing to be added to the PMP is a clarification of the project scope. What is the project going to deliver? What areas of the business does it impact? Which areas are specifically excluded? And what constraints are applied? This would initially be captured in the business case, and amended. And then captured in the Project Charter, and amended. And so on.

Because it gets amended so often, it's always a good idea to clarify it again in the PMP so that there are no assumptions and everyone is on the same page.

As an example, a project scope may say something like:

To deliver the ABC Software Inc customer service system to the Operations area of Bananas Bank. The system will be rolled out to the Customer Services team in the UK and the USA but not to the Finance teams. Finance will no longer be involved in the customer service process. The system will not be implemented in the International offices.

The existing system from Apples & Pears Limited will be decommissioned. All existing customer data will be migrated from the Apples & Pears Limited system to the ABC Software Inc system.

International clients' data will be migrated to the USA office.

One thing that is often missed is whether the implementation of the solution is included in the project. Or is it only delivering the product or system, and someone else will implement it? This should be made clear in the scope statement.

The scope may contain more detail, such as the type of data that will be included in the migration. However, it should not be *too* detailed, as that is the purpose of the Business Requirements Document, which we will come to shortly.

The thing we need to look out for here though is *scope creep*—or how to say 'no' and not get fired.

The first thing I ask a Project Manager for is their Business Requirements Document.

This tells me what the project is about and what it will fix—the scope.

I then check the project plan and the status reports looking for any disconnect between the documents.

I ask tricky questions like: 'Why are you working on xx when that's not in the requirements?'

And the PM will say, 'Oh, the Head of..xx asked if we could add that in.'

This is scope creep.

Why is it bad?

Adding in extra requirements and functionality costs more in development and testing time. If development and testing have been properly budgeted for at the outset, then adding the extra functionality will mean you go over budget.

And you may end up delivering something that doesn't meet the original need.

Which is the complete opposite to the approach taken in Agile project management, which we will look at in Chapter 11. There, the scope and requirements change constantly to accommodate the needs or requests (some may say whims, but not me, obviously!) of the customer.

However, you don't have to say 'no' to everything when working in the waterfall method!

This is why we have the change request process. Which allows stakeholders to make requests for extras, but in a controlled way.

Filling out the change request form and presenting the rationale to the project board for consideration of the potential impacts demonstrates it's something they really want/need. You wouldn't want to go through that laborious process if you didn't really, really want it!

Also, some PMs (again, not me, obviously) use phrases such as 'yes, we can add that into phase 2' knowing full well that there will never be a phase 2...all the while hoping that the person asking for the extras will move onto some other shiny, new exciting thing and forget all about their request. But, as I said, I would never do that.

Oh, look, sparkly unicorn!

Milestones & Project Plans

Now we are getting to the meat of the project! The next step for the Project Manager is to develop a high-level plan. This shows the key stages of the project from setting up the team, gathering requirements from the business, to developing or creating the solution, and implementing it before closing down the project. This may already be in the business case or PID (remember, the Project Initiation Document?). And, if so, it may need to be amended as decisions are made through the process of establishing the project.

But now it's time to get down to some detailed planning!

Planning Overview

The Project Manager is responsible for coordinating the overall project plan, although they will require input from most of the project team members. They will do most of the planning through project workshops where possible.

The ideal scenario for any Project Manager planning their project is to create a *left-to-right plan.* This means that they estimate the time required to complete each piece of work, then add them together, and, hey presto! They discover that the project is going to take three years, when they were given a six-month budget!

To overcome this, the Project Manager will look to see which tasks can be completed at the same time. They start scheduling work based on when it can start and finish. But then it starts to get complicated, because we recognise that some work has dependencies. Some things need to be completed before other things can start. For example, the Test Manager cannot begin testing the new system until the developers have built it. This creates a dependency and needs to be added to the RAID log, which we will cover shortly.

The Project Manager will identify the tasks that take longest and need to be done one after the other. This creates what is known as the *critical path* through the project. The critical path shows the minimum amount of time needed to complete the project. If a task on the critical path is delayed, or takes longer than planned, the timeline of the project will increase.

In the real world, left-to-right planning is actually considered a luxury. There is often an external deadline that needs to be worked to, such as the implementation of new regulations, or a system needing to be replaced before it expires. The deadline is set, and the plan has to be adjusted to meet that deadline. This often results in insufficient time for key stages of the project, such as planning and testing. Testing is usually the biggest casualty, as it comes nearer the end of the *project lifecycle*. If development work has taken longer than planned, then the testing schedule is always squeezed to make sure the deadline can be met.

To help with all of this planning and re-planning, most Project Managers will have access to a project planning tool, the most common of which is Microsoft Project. The Project Manager is able to enter each task or piece of work into this system and attach information to it.

As an example, a task may be to 'prepare initial project communications document'. The start date for this will be the first of the month. The Project Manager knows it will take three days to write the document and two days to obtain approval from the relevant managers. The task duration is entered into the project system as five days, which then shows it should be completed by the sixth of the month. At least that's the plan.

Now, this is a little bugbear of mine. Indulge me for a moment.... The number of times an earnest Project Manager has arrived at my door (as their Head of Change (HoC)), asking me to approve their 'fresh off the printer' business case, communications plan, or other project-related document... And if there's any chance I could look at it tonight? And it's already five minutes past 4:00 in the afternoon. And our working day is *supposed* to finish at 5:00 p.m. And I'm on my way to a one-hour meeting. Here's the thing. I am not a Test Manager. I cannot manipulate time. But, of course, they know I am often in the office until nearly 8:00 p.m., so *it's ok*.... The reason I am still in the office until 8:00 p.m. is because the aforementioned PMs don't plan in the necessary review time!

Please, for the love of all that is good in the world, give your document approvers, especially the HoCs who have to review everything, some advance notice that the document is coming. Tell them that you've emailed it (they have magical disappearing inboxes that make stuff invisible), and then give them a couple of days to actually read it. And, only after that time has elapsed, can you check in on their progress.

Nobody wants a PM checking in with them every two hours to see 'if you've had a chance to look at my document yet?' (actual quote from over 1000 Project Managers that I know personally). No, I have not, because it is on a pile with the other twenty-six documents that I need to read, one of which is a draft of your performance review, so please *be patient!*

Ok, rant over. Thank you for listening. Back to project plans...

The Project Manager can also attach resources to the project tasks. In the example above, on the communications plan, or comms plan for short, it will be completed by the Business Readiness Manager.

Once this information is entered, the task can be linked to other tasks to show dependencies. The subsequent task 'Issue initial project communication' cannot be completed until the previous task has been completed, which creates a dependency between the two tasks.

Once this piece of work has been completed, and the communication has been issued, we can say that a *milestone* has been achieved. We have delivered something, or some part of the work has been completed. The milestone activity is added to the plan as 'initial project communication issued'.

Note the difference in the wording structure of tasks and milestones. Tasks are written as 'verb noun', i.e., we are going to *do something*, and milestones are written as 'noun verb', i.e., *something* has *been completed*.

This helps anyone looking at the plan to identify milestones at a glance. To make it even easier, the MS Project system also recognises milestones when they are given a zero-days duration. This helps it to plot out the plan timescale in the form of a *Gantt chart*.

A *what* chart now?

When someone shows you a very complicated-looking chart,

usually printed on A3 paper, with lots of lines and little diamond shapes on it, then tells you it's their project plan, it's very likely a Gantt chart. Slowly back away from them. Tell them that you have an urgent appointment with internal audit. That will stop them from following you.

Gantt charts can be manipulated to show only the high-level milestones or to show every task in the project. Which can run to many pages on a big project. I once had a 400-page project plan. You have been warned. Back away. Audit...

Creating the Project Plan

One of the things that causes the most worry for new Project Managers is where to start with their plan. It can be quite overwhelming trying to document every task that needs to happen over a six-month period with a team of twenty people! But, if this is you, then don't worry. It's not as difficult as you may at first think!

The first thing to do is go back to the project scope and the Key Success Criteria (KSC) in the PID. These are the 'must do' deliverables for your project. Each one may lend itself to a workstream or a milestone. For example, if we need to deliver training to 500 people, the KSC for that could be:

Deliver system training for 500 people in the Customer Services team.

This is a significant piece of work, and we have already seen that the training part of the project will sit within the broader business readiness workstream. The Training Lead will create their own project plan, which will form part of the business readiness workstream plan, and then the overall project plan.

By doing this, we are starting to create the *work breakdown structure* (WBS) for the project. The project is broken down into workstreams based on key deliverables, workstreams are broken down into *work packages,* and work packages are broken down into milestones and tasks.

Got all that?

No, me neither! Let's have a drawing...

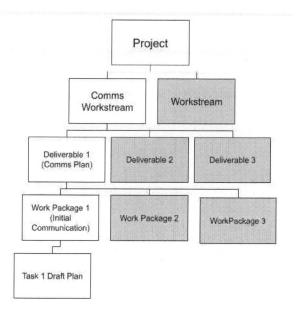

Example – Work Breakdown Structure

This example of the work breakdown structure (WBS) shows how we go from the overall project down to the comms workstream, then to one of the key deliverables, a comms plan. As part of the comms plan, we have several deliverables, one of which is the 'initial communication document'. Which is a work package with several tasks, the first of which is to draft the plan.

There are usually hundreds of work packages on each project, and the best way to work out what they are is to hold a detailed planning workshop. This is usually facilitated by the Project

Manager, who will be as happy as punch. Nothing gets a PM excited like a whiteboard wall and a bag full of Post-it® notes and coloured pens. In my project management days, you would often see me rushing from one meeting room to another with my little 'tidy bag' full of stationery goodies. Bliss!

Now that we have the basic project outline, we can fill in the remaining durations and resources, and, of course, any dependencies, and then we can let MS Project do its magic!

We pull out the key milestones and dates and create a 'timeline' picture to add to the PMP.

A very simple example is shown in Example 4.

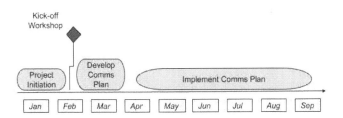

Example - Project Timeline

Budget or Cost Plan

A budget or cost plan is an essential part of project management, and a good PM will know exactly what costs are going to hit when.

So, what is this and how do I get one?

Cost estimates are included in the business case. Once approved, the estimates need to be firmed up as the project plan and resource plan are developed.

The costs need to be planned out month by month.

Example: On a twelve-month project, the contract PM costs start now. These are added to each month of the cost plan. The tester starts in June, so their costs are added to the plan from July (when the invoice is paid) on. The comms event is in October, so the cost is added in November. The supplier is due to be paid each quarter, etc.

Once these are plotted out month by month (I use a Microsoft Excel spreadsheet for this), then the Project Manager will have a fairly accurate idea of what should be coming out of the project budget every month. Most companies' Finance departments will provide a report of your *cost centre* expenditure every month, showing what was paid out against your project *cost centre code.* If you are ever responsible for a project cost centre, make sure that you examine the monthly report very carefully!

It is not unknown for random charges to appear that you have no recollection of and haven't approved. Which leads me on nicely to the *IT resource charging system*.

This is, in my humble opinion, one of the biggest wastes of corporate time known to man or woman. It's right up there with the appraisal system (more on that one later!).

Back in the mists of time, some very wise (?) people who worked in large organisations decided that the IT department must be able to account for their time, and, in doing so, be able to charge that time to other departments in the business. This is known as recharging.

Yes, you want a developer to work on your IT system? No problem, that will be two days' work, and we are going to charge your department budget 6 shillings for the privilege!

Your website page needs updating? We can do that. That'll cost you half a day at 20 shillings. Plus, you'll need it tested and uploaded, so that will be another three days and 120 shillings.

And we can do it in three months' time, because everyone is currently allocated to projects.

Now imagine if every department did that? The Sales team asks Marketing to develop a new product. Yes, of course, that will be 100 days and 700 shillings, please.

And in Finance...you want your monthly project cost report? Yes, here you go, that took me two days, and you can have it for 40 shillings. Thanks!

It's crazy, right? There are people who spend all their time just charging other internal departments. For things that don't actually cost real money.

But it gets worse. Because they then tell the IT department people that they have to be fully allocated. Except for training time. And holidays. Or sick days. And lunch. And going to team meetings. But, apart from all of that, fully allocated.

And what is the result? All of the IT people then spend around 10% of their time trying to find out what things they can allocate the other 90% of their time to. Minus holidays, lunch, and that training course they weren't invited to but turned up for anyway.

I'm sure if you bring this up with anyone in a senior position in IT, they will explain in great detail why it's necessary, and how it ensures they are providing a valuable service, allocating resources efficiently, blah, blah... Back away slowly, mention the internal audit thing we talked about earlier... Keep moving, slowly, slowly... no sudden movements. Otherwise, they will bill you for the conversation!

I'm sure there was a perfectly logical explanation for all of this at some point. I just have no idea what it was.

Thanks for indulging me once again...back to cost plans.

Now we have the cost plan mapped out month by month, we have our report from Finance which we have checked carefully for any random charges (IT!), and we've spotted some variances from the plan.

We now have something to pop into the 'budget' section of the project status report, a section which is mostly left blank. Because nobody is ever quite sure what's supposed to go in it. Well, now you know! We will compare how much we spent last month, and the total year to date spend (YTD), against what was in our original cost plan. And if there's a variance, then we can pop in some text advising why that is, and explain what we are going to do about it.

Oh, and don't forget to add the cost of the end of project party!

Resource Plan

Resource planning follows the same principles as cost planning. We map out month by month what project resources we need.

The business case *should* already contain an outline resource plan. If not, how can you estimate the cost of the project?

This outline shows who is needed on the project, when they need to start, and how long they are needed for.

It's usually shown as 1 FTE (full-time equivalent) or, if only needed for half their time, then 0.5 FTE, etc.

An example when using external contractor resources in the project may be:

Project Manager: 1 FTE x 12 months @ £500 per day

Architect: 0.2 FTE x 3 months @ £800 per day

But the plan must show all resources needed, including SMEs from the business, process operators needed for testing, and trainers, not just the external resources that need to be paid for. This is to ensure that they will be made available by each business area.

And, of course, don't forget to add in the cost of the *internal* IT resources if your business operates that model. IT at least tries to make it slightly easier to add their charges to estimates by creating an average per day rate, which applies to all of the roles they provide on projects. It's usually around £500 per day, whether it's for a developer or an Architect. Remember that this only applies to the *internal* resources though. You will need to add the cost of external resources at the rate you are paying for them.

Another thing to watch out for is where external resources are provided as part of a package deal.

It probably seems like great value at the outset, but their time on the project will be strictly limited. If you go over that time limit, a higher charge will usually apply. Make sure you understand the cost per resource per day in this case, as it can easily be double the day rate quoted in the initial estimate from the supplier.

Having the resource plan information in a simple format is

essential because, when (yes, when, not if) your project slips, then you can easily work out what that means in extra costs before going off to check that the resource will still be available in the new timeframe.

And don't forget to add in your own costs!

Project Key Performance Indicators (KPIs)

KPIs measure how well the project is going. Is it delivering on time, within budget, and to the right quality level?

There are many ways of determining whether it's on track. The simplest way is to check progress on the plan. Have you completed all of the tasks you were supposed to complete by the due date? A couple of days of *slippage* on a specific task may be okay, as long as a milestone hasn't been missed. If you have a lot of tasks and work packages, it may be more efficient to only track milestones, rather than trying to keep track of everything.

If things are starting to slip by more than a couple of days, they may need to be added to the RAID log as *issues*. With an explanation of what's gone wrong, the potential impact or knock-on effect of the delay, and any additional costs likely to be incurred.

The RAID log provides another valuable source of KPIs. How many unmitigated risks are there? How many open issues? This is a good indicator of project quality. If these are not being managed and kept up to date, there is a chance that the Project

Manager's time is being diverted elsewhere, perhaps in trying to manage the details of the project or resolving issues. It's very easy to get dragged into the details. Most Project Managers are aware that they need to rely on the team to deal with the details, to allow them to focus on the bigger picture and management of the project.

Another example of a commonly used measure is the *Planned Value* (PV) KPI. It can be used to determine if your project is on track, but it depends on having robust plans and estimates in place to begin with. It's calculated by:

%project completed x total budget, for example:

70% x £2.5m = £1.75m

What this tells us is that, if you are 70% of the way into the project (the duration), and you have spent £1.75m as planned, then all is well with the world. But if you have spent more than £1.75m, then your project may be in trouble. But don't panic yet! This measure depends on whether costs are running at the same rate every month, called the *burn rate*. If they are loaded upfront or towards the end of the project—check your cost plan—then this creates a different picture.

There are lots of other ways of measuring project success, but here's an important point...do not get so bogged down in tracking, measuring, and analysing your KPIs that you forget to keep your project moving along! The measures are only another tool to help you keep control of what's going on (or not going on, as the case may be!).

If you are lucky enough to have one, your PMO Analyst should be helping with this, and flagging things that need your attention.

And check with your Project Management Office, as they may already have measures in place that they apply to your project. Either way, they should be captured in your PMP and reported on through your status reports.

Project Key Success Criteria

The Key Success Criteria of a project are different from KPIs (which measure project *performance*) in that they are the essential *deliverables* that must be ticked off before the project can be said to be complete. The PMP will usually contain five or six specific and measurable outcomes that the end users and Project Sponsors base their *go/no go decision* on.

What? Are we go-go dancers now?

Not at all. It's not the '70s anymore! The project board and key stakeholders need to decide at the end of the project if they are happy for the new system, product, process, etc., to 'go live', or be implemented. And, rather than this be a discussion, or based on gut feeling, there is a checklist of items agreed upon up front that determine whether the project has done its job or not. We will look more closely at this process in more detail later, but these items are essentially the Key Success Criteria (KSC) of the project.

To develop the KSCs, we need to understand what is important to the end users or recipients. We can get this information in more detail from the business requirements gathering that we will look at shortly, but the business case should already give some indication.

A simple example of a KSC would be letters going out to customers. The KSC for this would usually be 100%. Which means that the letters must be 100% accurate during the testing process before they will be passed. The letters cannot go to the wrong addresses or contain the wrong customer information, especially as they may contain sensitive data.

And don't forget that a KSC must be based on *user outcomes*, not on achieving specific project tasks. You can complete all of the tasks in a project, but this doesn't mean that the users will be happy with the output!

Business Readiness, Communications, and Training Plans

Business readiness is the element of project management that differentiates projects from *successful* projects. It's not just about delivering the solution, it's about ensuring that the solution lands well with the target audience. It's such an important topic that we are going to give it its own chapter. Just remember that it still forms part of the PMP, along with a detailed stakeholder map.

The RAID Log

The next item in the PMP is the initial RAID log...a summary of the key risks, assumptions, issues, and dependencies captured at the kick-off workshop and added to as we go through the planning process. Just like business readiness, it deserves its own chapter, and we will look at it in more detail in Chapter 7.

Benefits and the Benefits Realisation Plan

Last, but not least, let's not forget the whole reason for doing the project in the first place! The PMP must include a statement of the agreed-upon benefits to be provided by the project. And it's helpful to have a plan showing how these will be realised.

For most projects, the benefits will be realised after the change is implemented. For example, an old system, which required new licences at a cost of £1m, can be scrapped as a newer and cheaper system was implemented at a cost of only £750,000. The project benefit is the £250k difference in costs, i.e. the saving that will be realised by the business not paying for new licences for the old system.

The challenge in this scenario is to make sure that this becomes a real savings, and that the money doesn't just get swallowed up by other expenses in the same department. One way of locking in the savings is to cut the department's budget by the amount that is to be saved.

Some projects may deliver benefits throughout the life of the project. Where an organisation is going through a restructure, for example, this may result in job cuts. As employees leave the organisation, their salary and other costs become savings, or project benefits. But, as in the example above, there must be a process in place to ensure that the savings are realised, either by having a headcount cap on departments or reducing the department budget.

It's more difficult to pinpoint and measure intangible benefits, but not impossible. These should form part of the project's Key Success Criteria (KSC) so that they can be ticked off once the project is complete. As an example, a KSC may require all staff to have received training on the new system. That is a measurable outcome. However, a good KSC would be that processing quality has improved. That sounds like an intangible outcome, but it can be measured if a quality standard or measure is put around it. The KSC could be that processing is 90% accurate within one month of implementation.

Project Managers should always try to encourage hard and fast benefits measures in their projects. It's the only way that they can demonstrate successful outcomes.

If a required benefit is 'increased customer awareness of a new product', for example, that cannot be easily measured. It's too woolly. But the benefit could be rewritten as 'a 10% increase in customer applications after implementation of the project'. Or a survey can be conducted post-implementation to ask customers if they are aware of the new product, with a comparison done at various intervals to test effectiveness of the project or campaign.

The Project Manager can do their best to ensure measurable benefits are delivered, but, at the end of the project, it's still the

Sponsor who is responsible for ensuring they were realised.

Chapter 5 Summary - What Have We Learned?

- What is included in the Project Management Plan
- Possible project team structures
- The project governance process and role of the project board
- Clarifying the project scope and how to avoid scope creep
- How to plan and an introduction to milestone planning, project plans, and the work breakdown structure
- How to create a budget and cost plan
- How to do a resource plan and what to watch out for
- An introduction to project Key Performance Indicators and Key Success Criteria
- The importance of benefits realisation and benefits realisation planning

6

Business Readiness, Communications & Training Plans

Project management can be planning the delivery of a new system or product or migrating data or implementing regulatory changes. In most cases, there will be a people impact from the change. The users or customers will need to understand what is changing, and what they need to do differently during the transition phase and in the new world.

What we need to recognise here is the difference between project management and *change management*.

Project management means that the system will work when you switch it on. It will do what it's supposed to do.

Change management means that the people who use it will know that it's coming and be able to use it properly. And they will have the resources to use it effectively. Customers should be unaware that there's been a change. Unless you want them to know.

Great change management means that everyone who is impacted by the new system is *excited* about its arrival and can't wait to use it. They know what to do with it and they rave about how great it is.

The alternative often results in a failed project and nobody wants that! The art of business readiness is exactly that, making sure that the business (and its customers) are ready for the forthcoming changes.

Let's figure out how we can make our project successful by, first of all, understanding the process that people go through when experiencing change.

The Change Curve®

You may have come across this before, perhaps in another guise, as it's closely related to the process people go through when experiencing grief.

Some projects can result in huge changes for the people impacted. People may have to learn a new way of working or may even lose their jobs.

Reactions will differ, as people are individuals, but their reactions are likely to follow a similar pattern. The rate at which they move through the pattern is the key to successful change management.

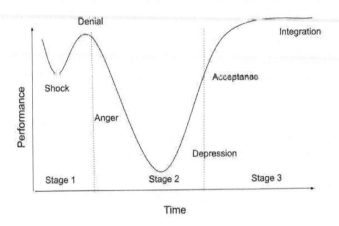

Example – Change Curve®

Psychiatrist Dr. Elisabeth Kübler-Ross illustrated the process as a graph resulting from her work on personal transition through grief in the 1960s[1].

She proposed that people initially react with shock to major changes.

Progressing to denial, then anger, as they understand how the change will affect them.

Depression in some form sets in as they realise that the change can't be avoided.

---

[1] You can find out more about the Change Curve® and the work of Dr Elisabeth Kubler-Ross at https://www.ekrfoundation.org/5-stages-of-grief/change-curve/

Most people will move out of this stage quite quickly, into acceptance, and then just 'getting on with it', i.e., integration.

The challenge for change managers is to make progression through these stages as fast and as painless as possible for the people affected. I will often say during the planning stages of the project that we must 'take the people with us on the journey'. Which sounds a bit cheesy, but, in reality, there is no point in leading an army onwards and upwards, then turning around to find you are climbing the hill all by yourself!

The best way to ensure you take people with you is through *engagement*. By involving people in discussion groups, listening to their answers, and making adjustments, they will feel heard. Overcommunicate what's going to happen, and how it will impact people. Tell them what they need to do to be successful going through the changes. And communicate with them in different ways. People absorb information differently. Some prefer visuals and want to know only the big picture. Some people like discussion, and some like details and facts.

Be conscious of your audience. I was previously responsible for rolling out a new *target operating model* (TOM) for a large team of accountants. The Communications Lead on the project had created a lively and colourful presentation to be delivered in various '*town hall*'-type meetings. They weren't particularly well received. And the retention rate for the information we shared was low during follow-up sessions. We very quickly realised that the approach we usually used would have to be altered to deal with this very specific group. We quickly arranged some small focus groups to find out what would work better. They didn't want glitz and glam presentations with lots of presenters. They wanted only the facts, and they wanted them written down. Okay, great, we could do that! We then created a weekly newsletter with all of the key messages for that week. It had, on average, a 97% open rate across the target audience. Which, in change management terms, is a great result! Give your audience the messages in a format that works for them.

Involving the people impacted in the decision-making process is always the best way when managing change. Nobody wants to have changes imposed on them, or to feel powerless when something major is going to change and they don't have any say in it.

It can be difficult when there are jobs at stake and the changes are particularly sensitive. If this is your project, then make sure that you have someone from HR advising on the approach and that the relevant social partners, union representatives, or others who represent the organisation's employees are brought into both the planning and delivery stages. They will be able to advise on the best way to tailor information for the audience, and can act as an early test group on sensitive information that cannot be released to the wider employee group until certain decisions have been made by the executive.

There is a lot to think about here, but the key is empathy...thinking about what you would want if the change was happening to you!

What is Business Readiness?

As we have covered above, business readiness is about ensuring that the people in an organisation are ready for the change. We can help them progress through the change curve quickly and easily by nailing our *business readiness plan* (BRP).

The BRP outlines our approach to communication, training, and support.

A great best practice approach to change management and business readiness preparation is outlined in the *ADKAR® model*, a framework for managing business change developed by a company called Prosci®[2]. It's based on the principle that, for an organisation to change, we must change one individual at a time. Which makes total sense, because we are all individuals, and we all like to be treated as such.

But, hang on, there are hundreds of users involved my project! I can't talk to each of them individually!

By following the steps outlined in the ADKAR® model, you won't have to. The key to success is involving leaders and managers in the organisation to help you achieve the right outcomes.

Let's look at it in more detail.

---

[2]   Find out more about Prosci® and the ADKAR® ® model at www.prosci.com

The ADKAR® Approach

ADKAR® stands for the five outcomes to be achieved through the change process:

A - Awareness D - Desire K - Knowledge A - Ability R - Reinforcement

Prosci® advocates that the steps need to be followed sequentially, and that we can't skip any or the changes won't stick.

Let's take a quick look at each outcome.

Awareness is about letting people know that a change is coming, why it's necessary, and what's in it for them. The best way to do this is by identifying the impacted users from the stakeholder mapping exercise (see below) and using the organisation's leaders and line managers to help deliver key messages.

Key messages should include the reasons for the change, including external drivers, and what bad stuff might happen if it's not addressed. It's a good time to get feedback and to allow the users to raise any concerns they have. This will not only let them feel that they have been heard, it may also uncover risks and issues that the project team hadn't previously considered.

Leaders and managers need to be fully informed and engaged before they can be asked to discuss the changes with their teams. They need to have credibility and be provided with as much information as is available at this point in time, so that they can tailor the messages for their teams.

They are also best placed to predict how individuals will react, and can tailor their coaching and support accordingly.

Desire is the next step, essentially explaining the changes at a more personal level, to encourage individuals to embrace the change.

Key at this stage is ensuring that incentives, performance management, and other organisational motivating factors are geared towards building desire for the change. The 'what's in it for me?' factor should point the individual towards recognising that the change will benefit them in some way. Again, leaders can support the delivery of these messages, and help to tailor them, to take into account the impacted individuals' personal circumstances, values, and motivators.

The biggest factor in achieving desire for change is the visibility, actions, and engagement of senior leaders, especially the Project Sponsor. If they are not seen to be taking the change seriously and creating opportunities for open and honest dialogue about the change, they are missing a trick. The more that individuals feel they are a part of the change, or at least being given the opportunity to talk about it, the greater the chance of creating the desire for change.

Leaders must also recognise that this isn't a one off 'tell them and then move on' situation. As more information becomes available, individuals' levels of engagement and desire to change will ebb and flow. The engagement process needs to continue throughout the life of the project.

I strongly recommend that the business readiness or training plan contains training for both Project Sponsors and for managers on how to lead their people through change, as they are the ones who will make or break the project. And they must build time into their schedules to support this.

They should also be aware of the level of change going on across the whole organisation and be sensitive to change fatigue. It's very easy for people to get overloaded when too many things are happening at once, and this can affect productivity. Especially when they perceive that the change may have a negative impact on them or their role. They can easily switch off and be unable to absorb new information which, again, will affect productivity.

Which leads us to the next step in the process, creating knowledge. This covers the information on required behaviours and skills needed to be successful in the new world, as well as process information and any changes in roles and responsibilities.

That's a lot of information!

Yes, it is. And how we tackle addressing that depends on the size of the gap. And this will differ across groups and individuals. Some individuals will be new to the organisation, and some groups will be more familiar with the new process, system, or tool than others.

The key to success here is understanding where the gaps are and providing the information in a variety of different ways that appeal to different audiences. And don't forget that this may mean two different sets of information. What needs to be done while going through the transition, and what needs to be done in the new world, as these two states may be different.

The other important factor is timing. People generally have a short memory for information retention. Offering training too far in advance risks them forgetting about it before they get a chance to use it. But they will also need sufficient time to practice before using it in the real world. The best way to ensure they retain information is to give them the chance to put it into practice in a safe environment first and to allow them time to iron out any issues.

Now we are moving full steam ahead into ability. Which Prosci describes as the difference between knowing how to do something and actually being able to do it.

The best way to build ability is to create a supportive environment where individuals have support from their managers, access to the tools and information they need, and the opportunity to practice without the fear of failure.

Where this support is missing, it's very easy for people to revert to the old ways as the new way of working is just too difficult. There are many barriers that stop people from adopting new ways of working. We've all been there and know that we respond to 'new stuff' differently. This comes from the existing habits that we already have, that are comfortable, and also any psychological blocks that we have.

For example, I hate getting a new phone. I need to learn how to do stuff in a different way. I can't be bothered to read the instructions. They are boring, and I am really just too lazy. I would prefer someone to show me on a one-to-one basis. Which is unlikely to happen. So, I fumble around for ages trying to figure out how to do the stuff I could do on my old phone without thinking. And probably never use half of the functionality of the new phone, because I haven't bothered to read the instructions. I acknowledge that I sometimes have a block about new technology. I am a laggard. Other people love new apps and new gadgets, the early adopters. We need to make sure our communication approach reaches everyone in the *adoption cycle*.

As long as we are aware of people's differences, we can build this into the training and communications solutions we offer as part of our business readiness planning. The goal is to ensure that all of our users achieve the ability outcome so that our project will be successful.

The final step in the process is <u>reinforcement</u>. We've put a lot of thought, time, and energy into delivering our plan. Now we need to make sure that the changes stick!

The best way to reinforce the change is to celebrate success. This doesn't necessarily mean that everyone heads down to the pub though. There are other ways to celebrate success that are linked to business outcomes.

For example, if you are working in an operations environment with a new system, you can apply quality goals to the teams' work. Celebrating success may mean that ten new customer applications have been processed with zero errors. Or that one individual has successfully completed their tests on the new system and achieved a recognised certificate or award.

And, on that note, another important point: the organisation's performance measurement and reward systems must also recognise the new ways of working. If people are still being targetted and measured against the old ways of working, there is no incentive for them to change.

Sometimes just a personal thank you from a leader is enough to reinforce the change for an individual. Sometimes they need to know that their performance bonus is linked to the way of working.

It's a good idea to keep checking in that the changes have been embedded, and one way to do this is through regular *temperature checks.* This can take the form of a short survey or focus group to find out how individuals are coping with the change and to identify any unresolved issues.

Project teams and managers have a key role to play here, in collecting feedback about what's working and what isn't, so that corrective action can be taken.

My final point on this approach is to make sure that you recognise what has been achieved at the end of the project. And that doesn't just mean the project party! Ask leaders to reinforce messages about what has actually been delivered and what the organisation has achieved as a result of the change.

Trying to change the behaviour, business culture, or work patterns of a large group of people is never easy. By following this recognised approach, you will give your project a better chance of success.

Stakeholder Management

We now have an understanding of how to take people with us on the change journey. We know what we need to do. We just need to figure out who we're going to do it with!

A great tool for helping with this is the *change impact assessment (CIA)*. This tells us who or what will be impacted by our project and to what extent. We can then figure out what each group or individual needs from the project to successfully adapt to the change.

Let's explore how to do a simple CIA.

Change Impact Assessment

The first thing we need is a template which highlights the key areas to consider. Your organisation may have its own, but, if not, here's an example.

Area of Impact	People Impacted	Degree of Impact (H, M, L)
Systems		
Processes		
Job Roles		
Performance Measures		
Reward		
Location		
Skills		
Culture/Behavioural Norms		
Business Tools		

Example – Change Impact Assessment

This table looks very straightforward, but, as you begin to use it in your organisation, you will realise it can become a fairly complicated activity. If you think about the many systems and processes that are involved in running your organisation, it can make your head hurt.

But don't worry. You don't need to do all of this by yourself. That's why you have, or are part of, a project team.

If you have SMEs in your team from different business areas, you can ask them to complete the template in their area. It's also a good idea to involve other experts, such as the business Architect or IT Lead. They will have a good understanding of what happens more broadly across the organisation and be able to assess what will be impacted or touched by the changes you are planning.

It's also a good idea to ask colleagues from HR, Finance, and Risk to complete this exercise, too, as they will have special expertise regarding what happens in the business and be able to save you a lot of time and worry.

Once the exercise is complete, there will be lots of 'people' identified as being impacted by the change, and to varying degrees, as high, medium, or low. The next step is to be able to group these into more manageable stakeholder groups.

For example, if you know that there are two groups of users who both access the customer accounts system, and the impact for them is 'high', then you can group them together to provide them with the same information and training.

However, if one group only uses the system occasionally, and the impact for them is 'low', then they may just need a light touch with a few communication emails to advise them that they will see a different screen when they login, for example.

Now that we understand who will be affected by our proposed changes, we can move on to managing them as stakeholders.

Stakeholder Mapping

We now know who is impacted by our project and, therefore, who we need to involve in the next stage of planning.

Can we just send them all the same information, or invite everyone to the same training course?

We could, but that wouldn't be the best use of resources. And it would probably annoy a few people at the same time.

A better way would be to think about where each group is in terms of their current engagement and understanding of the change, against where we *need* them to be.

Wait, that sounds a bit complicated.

Don't worry, I have another picture...

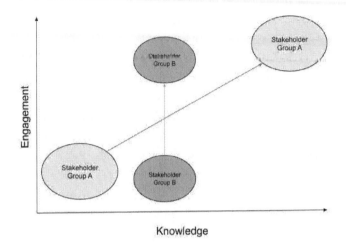

Example – Stakeholder Map

In this example, we have two stakeholder groups, A and B.

Group A includes employees whose area of the business is being reorganised, and their jobs are at risk of redundancy. At the moment, they know nothing about the forthcoming changes, and are not engaged in the change at all.

However, the changes will take a long time to implement, and we need them to continue doing their jobs during the transition period. We need them to become engaged in the change, and to understand why it's necessary. We can do that by giving them knowledge, or information, about the change, as we covered in the ADKAR® process above.

The journey from where they are now to where we need them to be is shown by the arrow, which effectively highlights the communication and training gap that we need to close. It represents their change journey.

Group B is made up of employees of the same business, who work in the HR department. They are aware that the changes are coming, but they are not fully engaged. The challenge here is to ensure they are on board with the changes and to help them support the rest of the business through the transition phase.

The communications and training plans are then based around how you will help them to make the transition to becoming more engaged.

The Communications Plan

We now have our audiences, and we understand what gaps they have. Using the milestone plan that we created earlier in the project plan as a framework, we can then create a journey for our stakeholders.

The stakeholder journey helps us to develop our communications plan and our training plan based on the overall project plan to ensure that communications are issued to different stakeholder groups at the appropriate time in the project.

For example, we know that we will have some SMEs from the business who will participate in User Acceptance Testing (UAT). They will need to have training on the new system before they can begin testing. They will have a different journey than other members of their department, who will receive their training and comms later.

The communications plan should contain different forms of communication to appeal to different audiences. As discussed previously, some people absorb information by audio means, some prefer visual methods such as infographics, and some prefer to read detailed instructions. It's important to understand your audience's needs before developing your communications plan, and you can only do that by engaging and understanding your stakeholders early on in the project.

A good Project Manager or Business Change Manager will tell the audience what changes are coming, tell them when the changes have arrived, and ensure they follow up to understand if their message has been received as intended.

A good way to achieve the latter is through temperature check surveys which ask three or four simple questions aligned to the Key Success Criteria of the project.

For example, some temperature check questions relating to training could be:

- Are you happy with the way the changes were delivered to you or your team?
- Did you receive the training for the new solution?
- Were you happy with the training?
- Was there anything missing from the training?

It's a good idea to do this early on in training delivery so that you can moderate the remainder of the training delivery based on this early feedback. It's also a good idea to build checks into various stages of the communications plan to ensure messages are being received as intended by the various recipient groups.

Most of the items in the communications plan should also have dependencies, or links, to other tasks or milestones in the project plan. This ensures that any slippage in the overall project is reflected in the communications plan. You don't want a communication going out telling people that the system is going live on Monday when it's actually been delayed by a month!

Training Plans

We have touched on the approach to training throughout this chapter. It's an essential part of any project after all.

And, for most projects, the training plan will be focused on delivering training towards the end of the project. It should contain technical training in relation to a new product or system, but, as we have covered above, there are other aspects of training that shouldn't be forgotten. Training on the process of change itself, especially for leaders and managers, will make the project land much better with the intended audience.

And, of course, as in the example above, we need to make sure we train the people who will participate in testing. Some may need training on the test process itself, as well as the new system or process. It's important that they fully understand what needs to be done, not just for the success of the testing, but because they will likely become change champions, sharing the benefits of the forthcoming change with their colleagues. Or, better still, they may become *super users*, who provide training and support during the early days of the transition and implementation period.

Some projects will use a train-the-trainer approach to save time in rolling out new processes or products. This involves the professional training manager training a group of employees on the new subject, and helping them understand how best to share this information with their colleagues. These newly trained trainers can then return to their own department and impart their new-found knowledge simultaneously, without the need for the training manager to visit every location.

Logistical Planning

There are a few other things that can be included under the banner of business readiness. These can be the more practical, logistical aspects of the project, such as organising desk or office moves, supervising desk drops of training and communications material (placing information directly onto each employees desk), or organising meeting rooms for individual staff meetings. And any special measures required for the migration/implementation, such as access to the office on the weekend. They are not the most glamorous of activities, but they still need to be attended to!

As more organisations move towards remote working these issues may become less of a problem, however organising project implementations remotely comes with a whole new set of challenges.

The Project Manager must work closely with the Business Readiness Manager (or the Business Leads if they don't have a BRM) to ensure that the business or organisation is set up for success and that nothing is left to chance when the project is implemented. Things will still be missed. It's never possible to account for every eventuality. But by taking a structured approach and thinking through the change in terms of the impact on individuals or different user groups, the project has the best chance of landing well with the intended audience.

Chapter 6 Summary - What Have We Learned?

- The difference between project management and change management
- The change curve and how it helps us to support people through change
- What business readiness is and why it's important for projects
- An understanding of the ADKAR® approach and how it helps us to deliver change
- How to map our stakeholders and use this to plan our communications and training
- What a change impact assessment is and how to do one
- What communications and training plans are and how to do them

- Other areas that we need to think about, such as logistics when we deliver change

7

Risk Management & The RAID Log

As we discussed before, RAID stands for Risks, Assumptions, Issues and Dependencies. I usually extend it and call it the ARI-ADD log, adding Actions and Decisions, so that I can keep everything in one place, usually on an Excel spreadsheet. Many PMO teams now use specialised project software, or file-sharing apps like Microsoft SharePoint, to keep track of things. It doesn't really matter where they are stored. Capturing them and then acting on them is the important thing.

And having all of this information in one place makes PMs slightly less crazy and makes it a little bit easier to write status reports.

I give each category its own tab on the spreadsheet. For example, with Risks, I will add the details in the form 'There is a risk that...', then add in who owns it (is responsible for managing it), the probability of it happening (high/medium/low), the potential impact (in terms of cost or delay), and what is being done to mitigate it, if anything.

The log is created early on in the project, perhaps during the initiation phase, and added to during the kick-off workshop. I usually hold a project workshop just on RAID items once we have an outline of the project plan. I will walk through the plan, checking dates and resources, and asking team members to call out any RAID items they can think of as we go along.

Smart Project Managers will also review their organisation's project *lessons learned log* to pick up insights from previous projects. And they will start their own lessons learned log early on in the project, as it's really easy to forget them once the project is delivered.

The organisation's log is usually maintained by a central project office, or PMO, and if you are lucky, they will walk you through it. Ideally, it will be organised in a way that you can filter it to see risks on projects similar to yours. It should contain a project reference number, project name, type of project, the 'lesson' and information on how it could have been prevented. It may also contain a key to certain types of risks, e.g. people risks, system risks, migration issues, etc., which will help you to filter it further, especially if it's a lengthy list.

Unfortunately, the work doesn't end after you have had a preliminary risk workshop and reviewed the lessons learned log. The RAID log will be added to throughout the project as new risks and issues are identified and it must be kept up to date.

What do I mean by keeping it up to date?

Each item in the log will have an action against it, unless the project board has agreed to accept it and take no action. If these are not checked and updated regularly, there is a good chance they will be forgotten about, and that's when things start to go horribly wrong!

Let's look at each of the log items in turn.

Risks

Project risks are something that may happen in the future and could have a negative impact on the project. They need to be recognised and addressed to avoid project failures, delays, and cost increases.

In addition to the items mentioned above, each risk should have a mitigating action against it with an owner and a due date. In my extensive project experience, neither the prayer nor the ostrich approach to risks has ever proven to be successful mitigating actions.

Let's have a look at how we might deal with a project risk:

There is a risk that the temporary Training Lead may leave the project before the training has been delivered because their contract is due to expire. This is also known as a *key person risk*, as, currently, no one else on the project has the skills or knowledge to be able to deliver this part of the project.

The risk owner: The Project Manager, as they are responsible for resourcing the project.

Probability of it happening: Low (or 25%)

Potential Impact: The project could be delayed by two weeks if the contract isn't extended or a replacement trainer can't be found. Project delays cost £5000 per day for ten working days (expensive resources not working) and cancelled training room bookings are £200 per day for ten working days, incurring a £52,000 budget hit if this is not resolved.

Mitigating action: The Project Manager will seek approval to extend the contract of the current Training Lead.

Action required by: (Add the date by which it needs to be resolved)

Where there is a chance that the risk *will* materialise, say, if mitigating actions aren't completed in time, or where mitigating actions just aren't possible, then it's a good idea to have a *contingency plan*. This means that you have an alternative course of action, a fallback position you can revert to, to minimise the impact on the project.

In the training example above, we could add using an existing in-house trainer as the contingency plan. They are not part of the project team, but it may be possible for the Project Manager to negotiate with the head of the training department to provide some additional resource if the situation becomes critical. If this is agreed upon, it can be added to the Risk log.

It's also a good idea to have an independent review of project risks from people who are outside of the project team. This doesn't necessarily mean that you have to use precious project budget to pay external consultants or auditors. Although they can be worth it, as they will bring a wealth of expertise and point out things you hadn't thought of.

It can sometimes be just as effective to use the resources already in your organisation. Having another Project Manager, or an experienced Head of Change or Projects, provide insight is useful. And involving experts in other areas, such as the Risk or Finance department, or even your own internal audit function if you have one is useful. They will bring a different perspective and may have been involved in similar projects before, either in the current organisation or with their previous employer. The thing that keeps most Project Managers awake at night is the thought of the unknown unknowns. You can't cover everything, but, in this case, many heads are better than one!

Assumptions

This is something that often catches people out in project world. It's the old 'I thought *you* were doing it' situation. The best time to flush these out is during walkthroughs of the detailed project plan. Gaps in the plan appear very quickly, along with assumptions about who's doing what.

Assumptions need to be validated, i.e., confirmed, with the party they relate to. It's all very well assuming that someone is going to do something for your project, but if you haven't let them know, and then tell them when you need it done by, then it's unlikely to get done.

And if it's something that you assume will be done by an external party, it might be better off in the dependency log and attached to an item in the project plan. This will make it easier to keep track of.

Issues

Issues always arise during the course of a project. Dealing with them is every Project Manager's bread and butter. We sometimes refer to a risk *crystallising,* which basically means that a previously identified risk has now become an actual issue and needs to be managed.

Every issue must be given an owner, someone who is responsible for managing it and ensuring it gets resolved. The Project Manager should regularly check on the progress of issue resolution, as any issue could easily escalate and derail the project.

Dependencies

As mentioned above, this is an action or outcome where we are dependent on an external party to complete something. This could be an activity carried out by a department not involved in the project, an external supplier, or even another project team.

They need to be advised that you have a dependency on them completing a specific task and when it needs to be completed by. I wouldn't rely on someone coming to tell me that they had completed something that I needed for my project either. I would check in with them regularly to make sure that it was going to be done on time. And, if not, I would have a contingency plan ready rather than be caught short.

Actions

I add actions to the log to provide a central point for actions arising from any project meetings. This avoids something key being lost in the minutes of the meeting and letting people off the hook because they didn't know about it! Whoever takes the minutes, or just the action points, should also make a point of sending an email with the action to the person responsible, unless there's another mechanism in place for letting them know about it.

Decisions

I add project decisions and a summary of why the decision was made, along with who agreed to it/owns it, in case this needs to be checked later, e.g., who approved an extra £50k spend on testing. It's always good to circulate these to the project team and interested parties on a regular basis, as it's a good way of making sure people know what's going on, or if something has changed.

Migration Risk Report

Although not strictly a RAID log item, I usually capture the details of the *migration risk* separately.

What's all this then? Are we moving to a different country?

Not at the moment! But we may be migrating data from one IT system to another. And this is the riskiest time of the project for any business. For most businesses, the risk can be minimal. If something goes wrong, they just revert to the old system.

So, what's the big deal?

For some financial services businesses, e.g., banks, asset management, or life and pensions companies, making a mistake during this stage of the project can end up being very costly.

Where shares or other assets are being bought and sold, or there are currency exchange requirements when placing a trade for example, and a transaction is carried out at the wrong time, or with the wrong information, it can end up costing the business millions.

Imagine a scenario when a client calls up to sell shares, as they have seen that the share price is high that day. The agent is unable to complete the transaction because the old system is closed down and the new one isn't working properly. The next day, the price drops considerably, but the agent *is* able to complete the transaction. How happy do you think the customer is going to be? Not very! They have potentially lost a healthy profit on the transaction because of the delay in selling. And the business may be liable to cover the difference between the selling price that *could* have been achieved and what was *actually* achieved.

The Migration Manager will be responsible for ensuring that there is a cut-off point for all transitions before the migration begins (usually 5:00 p.m. on a Friday until 9:00 a.m. on a Monday). Different transactions may have different cut-off points. The Business Readiness Manager is responsible for ensuring that the business is aware of this.

Key customers may also be advised that there may be a service disruption and a subsequent delay in processing any transactions. If they know that there are significant transactions due to take place on that Monday, or even into Tuesday, these will be captured in the migration risk report with various scenarios given around the extent of any potential losses.

I always ask the Project Sponsor and senior business manager to acknowledge receipt of this report and that they accept the risk. Because, in these regulated businesses, if something goes wrong, they must be able to demonstrate to the regulator that they were aware of the potential risks and that the risk was being managed.

This information will be superfluous to the needs of most readers, but it's something that is very often neglected in project management, and I think that it's worth calling out.

We are now in a great place with the project. All of our set up activity has been completed. We have a plan, and we know what could potentially go wrong.

Let's do it!

Chapter 7 Summary - What Have We Learned?

- What is included in the RAID, or ARIADD, log and why they are important
- How to identify, track, and manage risks, issues, assumptions, actions, decisions, and dependencies
- What is a migration risk report and why you may need one

8

Executing the Project

Wow! That was a lot of upfront planning! Planning and preparation are everything in project world, and this time taken upfront to plan will serve us well going forward.

But now it's time to move onto the nitty gritty detail of getting the project moving and making things happen!

There are different approaches to this stage of project management. The traditional waterfall approach, where everything happens sequentially, and the goal is to deliver what was asked for by the customer or user at the outset.

Or the more recent Agile approach, often used in software development, where the development work is carried out and tested in *sprints* and adapted to suit the customer's changing requirements as the project goes along. Don't worry, we won't be running anywhere!

The approach we are focusing on in this book follows the

waterfall approach in the main, although a lot of the principles, e.g., managing risk, apply regardless of the methodology used.

We will look at Agile project management methodologies in more detail in a later Chapter, as it's becoming increasingly used by organisations for all project types, not just for software development.

Business Requirements & Data

In the waterfall approach, the first thing we want to look at is the business requirements. Our trusty Business Analysts (BAs) will sit with the Subject Matter Experts (SMEs) to understand the current processes, the 'as is' situation, and then the 'to be' scenario. The difference between the two is the requirements, i.e., what needs to be done to change from one situation to the other. This process is often referred to as gap analysis.

This can involve process changes and outcomes from systems, but should remain within the scope of the project and ensure that the project Key Success Criteria (KSC) are achieved.

An example of a current process could be:

Input customer address to screen 1 of Customer Management System.

In the new system, which is set up differently, it could be:

Input customer address to screen 2 of Customer Service System

Post code must be added before allowing continuation to screen 3.

The BAs will draw up lots of *process maps* to show the flow of data through an organisation, or to show the steps carried out by employees.

They may also be responsible for capturing items for the *data dictionary*, a repository for all the types of information used in the systems that could be impacted by the changes. This may seem like overkill, an unnecessary step that just makes things more complicated, but it's one of the most frequent areas of failure in testing.

I witnessed this early on in my project career when a large bank was migrating customer's mortgage accounts from a building society they had acquired over to their own system. The migration tests kept failing, and nobody could figure out why. Eventually some bright spark noticed that the building society role numbers (the equivalent of an account number) were eleven digits long. And that bank account numbers are only eight digits long. And when you try to squeeze eleven digits into eight spaces, the computer says, '*No*', and the test fails. Or it only captures the first eight digits of the number. Which isn't helpful when a lot of account number start with the same numbers.

It would have been better to capture the information as:

Mortgage account number: 8 character spaces, numeric only

then, someone reviewing it from the building society team,

would have perhaps noticed the error.

The data items that cause the most problems in these situations, though, are customer addresses. Where a company has acquired customers from another business, through a takeover for example, the original company may have captured address information in this format:

7
   Castle Terrace
   Edinburgh
   EH1 1BC

But the new company's system is set up to capture the address in the format:

7 *Castle Terrace*
   Edinburgh
   EH1 1BC

When the data is migrated over the '7' will likely be lost and the test will fail.

This is the level of detail that needs to be captured when completing business requirements to ensure that things go smoothly during testing. It's not easy and requires a lot of patience to ensure nothing is missed.

Build/Development

Once the requirements have been captured, it's time to hand these over to the IT team, who will produce a *functional specification document* for the system changes. This is an outline of what changes are required in the system requiring development or configuration work to ensure that the system works the way that the customer wants it to. This work is often done by System Analysts, but they are not usually part of the project team. On larger projects, there may be an IT Lead or IT Project Manager who is responsible for liaising with colleagues in IT and ensuring they understand what needs to be done.

For non-IT projects, it may be a case of sharing the requirements with an external supplier, e.g., with a marketing agency, for an advertising campaign, or with a manufacturer if they are producing a new product.

This may take the form of a contract, *statement of work,* or product specification.

Once the development work is complete, it's time to test it out and see if everything works as planned. But don't hold your breath, as something always goes wrong at this stage, and that's okay. Better to find out the issues now before the new system goes live or the new products are sent out to customers.

It's worth noting at this stage that this is one of the main points where Agile and waterfall project methodologies differ. In Agile, only a small part of the work will be completed before it's tested, modified, and tested again. This is called a sprint. In the waterfall approach, most of the work is completed before the testing phase begins.

Testing

Before we can launch our new system or product on our unwitting colleagues and customers, we need to test that it works as expected. There's a lot to cover here as it's such a huge subject, but for the purposes of this book we only need to have a high-level understanding of what's involved and what the various test phases are.

The Test Manager is responsible for coordinating all of the testing and will work closely with the Project Manager and IT colleagues to create the test plan once the requirements are understood and the milestone plan has been agreed to.

The first thing they need to do for an IT project is either book out the test environment or make sure one is built. This isn't as scary as it sounds. It just means that they need to replicate the same systems that are used in the real world, the *live environment*.

This means that everything can be tested safely without fear of disrupting the day-to-day business. Then we need to pop some dummy data into it, which is similar to the data we use in the actual system. Where this isn't possible, we may use real customer data, but we have to *anonymise* it to comply with data protection laws. We generally don't have our customer's permission to use their data for our own purposes, so we change some of it, perhaps the name and address and date of birth data, so that the information we are interested in, e.g., transaction information, can't be linked back to an actual customer.

Once we have our test environment set up and we have our data ready, the next thing is to check the data and do a *data cleanse*. Everybody ready for a good cleanse, yes? Ha ha, nobody wants to do a cleanse but it's ok, we are not going for a kale and broccoli shake any time soon. It just means that we need to check the data that we currently hold for any gaps, text that doesn't fit the correct format, or that's in the wrong place. This work might be done by a Data Analyst who is a specialist in knowing what can go wrong when working with a lot of data.

That's a lot of work before we get started though? Yes, because using data with errors in it is typically where our tests fail.

Taking the customer address again as an example, if the address box has only fifty character spaces and there are addresses with, say seventy characters in them, the system won't be able to load them into the new system, and the tests will automatically fail.

We now have our data. It's all good—as far as we know—so we can start the testing process!

At a high-level, we have two kinds of testing: non-functional testing and functional testing.

As we covered earlier non-functional testing means that we switch the new system on, and it works, and it's fast enough, etc. We all want to avoid the pain of the swirling circles on our screens!

Non-functional testing is broken down into different tests to check for different things, generally:

- **Performance testing** – does it run fast enough?
- **Load testing** - will it work with lots of users logged in simultaneously?
- **Failover testing** - will the back-up system work if it crashes?
- **Compatibility testing** – does it work with other applications?
- **Usability testing** – is it easy to use?
- **Stress testing** – will it work under pressure, with a lot of data or users?
- **Maintainability testing** – is it able to update?
- **Scalability testing** – is it able to scale up or down as user requests vary?

I remember once explaining to my mum that we were about to start stress testing on my project. She was really worried I was going to fail. Bless her. I think it's a good job that we don't test PMs or Test Managers for stress at this point in the project... I'm not sure many of us would pass!

The second is functional testing, which test whether, when we input some information, we get the expected result or outcome as described in the requirements or acceptance criteria. For example, if we wanted a system that showed all of the accounts a customer had, or everything they ever bought from our company, we would put in the client's account number and their information would show up. Without anything missing and without adding in another customer's information.

Types of functional testing include:

- **Smoke testing** - the initial check of the test environment to ensure it works, sometimes called build verification testing
- **Sanity testing** - ensuring that all the critical functionalities are working
- **Regression testing** - rechecking to make sure that everything still works after we have added new code or fixed bugs
- **Integration testing** – making sure individual modules of the system still work when they are joined together
- **Interface testing** - a subset of integration testing ensuring data exchanges and commands between different components work as expected
- **System test** - a full check to ensure that all components of the system work together as expected in as close to the real-world scenario as possible
- **User acceptance testing** - ensuring that the processes written by the Business Analysts can be followed and that the system works as expected for the users (this testing usually identifies missing steps in the process or where there has been a misunderstanding between SMEs, Bas, and developers)

Sanity testing...ha ha.. As above re the stress testing! Yes, let's not test the PMs for that either....

Once all testing has completed and the *User Acceptance Criteria* (UAC), i.e., the 'must haves' of the new system, have met the required quality standard, the new system will be ready for implementation. The next step is to implement the migration plan.

Migration

It's time for the Migration Manager to step into the spotlight!

Their main responsibility throughout the project has been creating a minute-by-minute (yes, it's very detailed) plan for the transition period to switch on the new system.

In most cases, the plan will start after business hours on a Friday to minimise disruption to any live systems. Most people will, more than likely, have had a notice from their bank at some point saying that their systems will be unavailable during a period over the weekend for maintenance. This is generally when new systems are being switched on, or data is being transferred from an old system to a new one.

There are a couple of logistical points to think about before we move into the detail of the migration. You may think these things are obvious, and good on you! You would probably make an excellent Business Readiness Manager! But, unfortunately, not everyone is as clever as you and there have been, well, let's just say, some *unfortunate incidents*.

The first one is about ensuring that the people working on the migration can access the office building at the weekend. You don't want to arrive at the office at 9:00 a.m. on a Saturday morning to find a group of very annoyed IT types waiting out in the rain because nobody organised weekend access and their passes don't work.

The second is realising that many modern office buildings have movement sensors in place after normal working hours. Which means that the lights go out regularly, and you will see people start frantically waving their arms around before finally resorting to standing up and walking in a circle around their chair to trigger the lights to come on again.

Then there is the absence of air conditioning on the weekends. Which is even worse than waiting in the rain, because there's not much you can do about it. If you work in a modern office block and you've experienced an aircon failure, then you will know how hot these glass buildings get with lots of computer equipment churning away for hours. And then it starts to get a little bit sunny outside. And, before you know it, the entire team is melting.

Try to negotiate with the Facilities department to switch the air-con on for your migration weekend. Otherwise, you are facing a very long weekend, stuck in a greenhouse-type environment with a bunch of gently steaming (from the rain), slightly sweaty, and extremely grumpy developers. Add a few cans of Lynx deodorant into the mix, and, trust me, this is not how you want to spend your Saturday!

Usually, while all of this is taking place, the PM steps into a support role, with the Migration Manager calling the shots. The PM will be holding regular calls with the sponsor and other project board members to update them at significant points over the weekend, especially in relation to whether Key Success Factors/User Acceptance Criteria are being met or not. There will typically be a few decision points built into the plan throughout the course of the weekend, and the great and the good will convene (usually by conference call) to decide whether things are on track and the implementation can progress, or whether they need to back out and fix some issues.

Sometimes the Head of Change will hover nervously in the background, especially if there have been some issues during testing, or the timeframe for finishing the migration is especially tight.

However, I know from experience, that standing over a developer at 2:00 a.m. while he retypes a key piece of code isn't actually very helpful. Apparently. The best thing you can do in this situation is phone for pizza, or go to the 24-hr supermarket for more cola and crisps. Or doughnuts. Doughnuts are popular. And coffee. Lots of coffee. And maybe a couple of cans of air freshener or deodorant if the aircon issue hasn't been resolved...

Despite the best laid migration plans, there have been many high-profile migration failures, especially in the banking arena, where systems have crashed and cash machine networks have gone down. But you can rest-assured that the people working on these projects really try to account for any eventuality. There's nothing more soul-destroying than watching your already exhausted team having to rally for another few hours to fix something that hasn't gone well.

In most cases, things will go according to the plan, and everyone can go home happy, have a couple of drinks (and a shower!), and a good night's sleep. However, if something isn't quite right, and the User Acceptance Criteria haven't been met, then we invoke the back-out plan. Which basically means we switch off the new system and revert to what was already in place.

And then, depending on how much rework and retesting needs to be done, we get to do it all again on a subsequent weekend!

Once the new system is finally live, the project team can have their celebratory party. These generally start off with great enthusiasm, but quickly deteriorate as exhaustion sets in after many long days to get to this point. And previously neglected partners start to text asking for an estimated time of arrival!

And then it's on to the next project as most of the team will very quickly be allocated to another project. Great friendships are often made on project teams as they have to work very closely together during an intense and often stressful period of time. It can be a bit disconcerting when it's all over and everyone goes their separate ways. Everyone promises to meet up again soon, and to keep in touch but it's never quite the same as when you are all in the thick of things together.

Now, dry your eyes and let's have a look at how we close down the project!

Chapter 8 Summary - What Have We Learned?

- What's involved in starting the project, the execution phase
- What are business requirements and how we get them
- The importance of data management in projects
- What happens in the development or build stage of the project
- The different types of testing and what they are used for
- What happens during the migration or go live phase of the project

9

Closing the Project

This area of project management is probably the most neglected. Quite often, Project Managers are asked to start work on their next project before they have completely finished the current one.

But it's an important part of the project and, if nothing else, it can provide a lot of valuable insights to make sure the next project goes well.

Which leads us nicely onto the next topic...lessons learned!

Lessons Learned

As mentioned earlier in the book, the lessons learned log is just that. A place to store valuable insights about what worked well and what didn't go so well. What would we do differently next time? The first thing is, it's not about finger-pointing or allocating blame. The focus here must be on learning and figuring out how things can be done differently next time.

The Project Manager will usually organise a lessons learned workshop at the end of the project with representation from each area of the project team, someone from the PMO, users/recipients of the new system or product, and, of course, the Project Sponsor.

When there has been a major issue on a project, or it has gone massively over on time or budget, there may need to be a detailed workshop on a specific aspect. The PM and PMO will want to drill down into the detail to fully understand what went wrong and whether the issue could have been avoided.

This all provides useful information to future PMs, who can avoid making the same mistakes or being caught out by an unexpected occurrence. *But only if they read the lessons learned log!*

Most lessons learned logs get updated by the PM at the end of the project, but they never review them before they start their next project. There can be some hidden gems in these logs. It's really worth an hour or two to have a look through, in case you find something that might save you days of wasted time on your next project.

Closure Report or Post-Implementation Review

The post-implementation review may be carried out by the PM, but it's sometimes better to have the review conducted by an independent third party. This could be someone from the PMO, someone from audit who has expertise in projects, or even another Project Manager.

PMs are often a bit nervous about this exercise, as they are worried it's going to point out loads of things they did wrong or missed. That's not really the purpose of the exercise though. Its real purpose is to capture the approach to the project, detailing what was eventually delivered, and highlighting any differences from what was initially planned. This is particularly important in technology projects, as people often need to refer back to the documentation if the same system needs to be worked on again in the future.

There will be recommendations on what could have been done differently, and these will also be added to the lessons learned log, along with details of things that were done really well.

Any work that hasn't been completed as part of the project will also be highlighted here. There should be information on how that outstanding work will be completed, or whether it's just not going to be done. Quite often, there will be some tasks left for the users or receiving business area to pick up to be completed as part of business as usual (BAU) activity.

Closing the Cost Centre

Once the project is finished and all invoices have been paid and staff costs are no longer being recharged to the project cost centre, the PM should instruct Finance to close the project cost centre.

This is quite often forgotten about, and things can inadvertently be charged to a project that finished months before.

If you are working on the project and don't want to end up trying to unravel a cost report months after the project ends, then make sure to contact your Finance friends and let them know not to accept any more charges against the project code.

Other Close-out Activities

The Project Manager should ensure that all of the items in the RAID log are closed out before saving a final version of the log in the project shared drive. All of the project documents should then be sent to the PMO for archiving, in case anyone needs to check anything on the project in future.

Another thing to do at this point is to ensure that all contracts have been terminated. This may relate to third-party suppliers who were engaged purely for the duration of the project.

But it can also relate to temporary workers or consultants who were engaged to work on the project. I regularly see this not being managed well, and, like everything else in project world, communication is the key. Nobody likes to be in a situation of uncertainty, and the Project Manager or Head of Change should meet with those temporary workers around a month before the end of their contract or project to let them know that they will not be required beyond the end of the project. This gives them the opportunity to start looking for their next role and avoids any unnecessary uncertainty.

Benefits Realisation

Settle in people, this is one of my favourite soap box issues...

Every project must have a clearly defined business case, which shows specific, measurable benefits.

The business case cost-benefit analysis shows what it might cost to achieve those benefits.

The project benefits can be tangible, i.e., in pounds...saving money, selling more products, increasing market share, etc.

Or intangible, such as improving customer service or employee satisfaction, or legal compliance. But these can also have tangible financial value. You can put a value on avoiding a huge regulatory fine, for example. Just do a Google search on what fines have been applied to competitors recently for messing up the same regulation!

But sometimes in project world, we get so involved in the details of projects that we forget why we started them in the first place.

Although some people forget even before that.

I have had business cases asking for money that didn't have any benefits in them at all. Why would we do a project if it wasn't going to deliver any business benefit? And these weren't 'must do' projects for legal or IT reasons—although these have benefits too. These were discretionary projects—building a new system or adding a new product—just because someone thought it was a good idea.

But the most common point of failure for organisations is not following up on the benefits plan after the project ends. They spend all the time, money, and effort to deliver the project, and then nobody follows up to check that what was supposed to be delivered has actually been delivered.

Now some of the deliverables will be checked in the post-implementation review. Does the new system have a bright red button? Does it churn out the correct report when you press go? And so on...

But, quite often, the slightly inflated financial benefits that were wafted around at the Project Investment Board are not delivered, and not checked.

How do you ensure these benefits are actually realised? Cut the department budget by the benefit value? Remove headcount from the team that should now be more efficient?

This is an ongoing challenge for our colleagues in the Finance department, but it's one that should definitely be on the agenda of any organisation's management meetings.

For those working in project world, if you really want to make a difference in your business, then focus on this.

There's no point in spending money, and working for years, to end up not getting the result!

Our project is now closed and it's time to recognise and celebrate the team's achievements.

It's good practice to recognise any stand-out individual contributions on the project, as well as the overall contribution that the team and project have made to business success. Not only does this encourage and motivate members of the project community, but it also serves to underpin the benefits achieved through the project implementation, demonstrating that the project has worked.

Many projects, especially IT changes, are carried out behind the scenes, and most of the organisation will never be aware of them. However, where there is a significant benefit to the organisation, or improvement in ways of working, for example, then it's a good idea to present an overview of the change to the rest of the organisation. This is traditionally done as a presentation at a company meeting, through an in-house newsletter, or sometimes as a display within the company's office.

The purpose of this is two-fold. It shows that the organisation can successfully deliver change. And it shows the employees, and potentially clients as well, that the company is improving and innovating, and realising significant benefits from its change agenda.

Chapter 9 Summary - What Have We Learned?

- What the lessons learned log is, why it's needed, and how to create one
- What the closure report or post-implementation review is and what is in it
- Things to close out at the end of the project
- Why benefits realisation is important and how to track benefits

10

Monitoring & Controlling the Project

The project has been delivered, everyone is happy and thinking about their next project. But this didn't just happen by chance. There were processes and controls put in place to make sure things stayed on track and that the project delivered what it was supposed to.

Let's have a look at what's involved in keeping everything under control.

The PMO

Many organisations have a central Project Management Office (PMO) to provide governance and a centralised reporting capability for their project portfolio. Some larger programmes and projects may even have their own PMO.

The PMO will maintain the project governance and methodology (the rules and standard) and ensure that the rules are followed. They usually maintain a copy of all key project documents, e.g., the business case and weekly status reports. They will use these to collate a central report for the organisation's senior management.

However, they are not just document collators. The best PMOs add value by providing analysis and quality assurance on projects.

They will often attend project meetings or check the meeting minutes for decisions that may impact the costs or benefits of the project and will check to ensure that these have been reported in the status report. And that the necessary change control paperwork has been completed if there is a shift outside the accepted variance levels.

They will usually run the organisation's Project Investment Board, or similar management meeting, to review all projects, and to review change controls covering requests to extend timelines, budgets, etc.

They may also work with Project Managers to analyse project plans and RAID logs to check for any issues and to make suggestions about anything that may have been missed.

As well as having sight of what's going on across all of the organisation's projects, they generally have long memories and can advise on lessons learned from previous projects. And they are a great resource for identifying project dependencies across the organisation. They see everything and can join the dots. It's not the first time that a project train wreck situation has been averted because someone in the PMO spotted two competing priorities, or a delay that was going to impact another project.

Good Project Managers work closely with their PMO to make the most of their knowledge. And to keep on their good side when they need a status report deadline extension. I have heard that buying chocolate for the PMO Manager may influence this latter point, but I wouldn't know personally, as obviously, I would never stoop so low as to try that for myself. Because my status reports are always on time. Obviously. Always.

Which leads us nicely to the next section.

Status Reports

Status reports are the bane of a Project Manager's life, but, unfortunately, a necessary evil. Unless your organisation has invested in real-time technology for recording project events, then your Project Manager will be required to complete a regular status report.

The status report gives an update on where your project is against the plan, along with details of any issues that have arisen, and what you are doing to address them. It's usually shared with the PMO and the Project Sponsor, but it may also be made available to members of the PIB or other senior managers in the organisation.

If you are ever wandering around an office late on a Thursday night and see a bunch of Project Managers hunched over their keyboards (occasionally waving their arms to get the lights to come back on), they are not being particularly conscientious (or having a stroke). It's because their status reports are due in to the PMO on the Friday.

Why is this such a difficult task?

I'm glad you asked!

Normally, the status report would be quite simple to complete. You give an update on what the team have achieved that week, including any milestones achieved (or missed), highlight any new risks or issues identified, pop in the latest costs vs budget numbers from your lovely friends in Finance. And you give it a colour—a RAG status - Red, Amber, Green. Status reports are given a colour to indicate whether everything is going well (green), or not so much (red). The middle ground (amber) is seen as a safer option, but is actually a quagmire of confusion and uncertainty.

You fill in the blank template with all of the relevant information, and there we have it. A new status report. Job done.

Or is it? What could possibly go wrong?

Politics. That's what. Unfortunately, most of the PM's time is spent trying to carefully word things to ensure that they report an issue, but they don't set off any alarm bells and cause a major panic. Or throw anyone under the bus.

If you get a call within three minutes of issuing your status report, then you have probably failed at this.

Then there is selecting from the rainbow of colour opportunities which will define how well your project is going. The whole RAG (red, amber, green) status thing. Or 'Fifty Shades of Amber', as I like to call it.

Nobody, but *nobody*, wants their project to be reported as '*red*'. Even if your project is on *fire*, over budget by £1m and six months late, there is still a way of rationalising amber. Or your Project Sponsor will find a way to convince you to find an appropriate shade of amber.

And this is where the political, influencing, and communication skills of great PMs kicks in. Because sometimes a project is *red*. Bright, glowing, fire-engine red. And it needs to be called out in such a way that, of course, no one is to blame. It's just project life.

Except for third-party suppliers. They can always be blamed. And frequently are. Even when they left the project months earlier, they can still be blamed for things.

Or Fred, the project guy. He's a bit useless, messes stuff up a lot, and never turns up to meetings. Nobody has ever actually met 'Fred'. But he's been around so long that they don't want to show their lack of ignorance, or lack of interest in the rest of the team, by admitting that they don't know who Fred is. But he gets blamed for a lot of stuff. And is on the verge of being fired at least twice a week for his incompetence.

Of course, Fred doesn't actually exist. But, when things aren't going well, and you need to focus on the solution, it's a lot easier to just blame 'Fred' than to get into a whole investigation about who actually did what. Or didn't do what. There will be plenty of time later for that, but, for now, something needs fixing, and fast. And, anyway, Fred has broad shoulders. Or so I've heard. I wouldn't know. Never met the guy. I think he got fired...

But back to the status report and calling out the issues. In the long run, it's always better to call out the issues and deal with them then and there. It might not make you very popular with the great and the good, but at least if it's out there, the issues can start to be addressed. And, in my experience, one issue often leads to another and, before you know it, the whole project starts to unravel. Call it out, explain what you're doing to fix it, and move on.

Every problem, issue, or risk creates an opportunity for someone to shine, to step in, and save the day. Just don't ask Fred.

Chapter 10 Summary - What Have We Learned?

- The role of the PMO in monitoring and controlling projects
- The purpose of the status report and how to complete one
- How to navigate the politics of status reporting

11

Agile Project Management

What is Agile? I debated whether to include a section on the Agile project management methodology. Because, really, it's just another tool in the Project Manager's toolkit, albeit one that requires a significant change in mindset around how to plan and monitor project activity. But there has been such a focus on it while I was writing this book that I thought I should at least try to explain some of the terminology.

The Agile approach to project management is really a collection of methodologies focused on delivering value, optimising efficiency in the delivery of project activity, specifically build or development work, and using a team of people to bring continuous improvement to the project approach.

Agile evolved in response to the need for greater success in the delivery of software development projects. It was created by developers, rather than Project Managers, and therefore tends to be lighter on planning and control activities than other more traditional approaches. Essentially, the waterfall approach was taking too long, making software obsolete by the time it was delivered. Waterfall also works on the basis that the requirements and scope are agreed up front and can only be changed if, and when, hell freezes over.

And waterfall doesn't really lend itself to building something that the customer doesn't know is even possible, or can't envisage yet. They think they know what the problem is, but they may not know what they want as the solution. Because they're not aware of everything that's possible.

Imagine the scenario where a customer is asking for a smaller, more portable set of encyclopaedias. He or she may ask you to make the books with smaller print, on lightweight paper, and to put them in a carry-bag for easy transport. They have no idea that every encyclopaedia ever written can be made available to them on a gadget that's the size of a bar of chocolate. It's an extreme example, but you get the idea.

Four values emerged while the creators of the Agile methodology were wrestling with these issues and other issues. These values formed the basis of the Agile Manifesto3:

- Individuals and interactions over processes and tools
- Working software over comprehensive documentation
- Customer collaboration over contract negotiation
- Responding to change over following a plan

We should just forget everything you've been telling us in the last few chapters, then?

142

Well, not exactly. It's horses for courses. I'm not suggesting that an Agile approach is the panacea for all projects. Let's not throw the baby out with the bathwater. It has its place, especially for software development, but more and more organisations are attempting to apply the principles to all or most of their projects. Or a hybrid of the two methodologies.

Say what, now?

Yes, you read correctly. It's possible to have the overarching project run as a waterfall project, using Agile principles, and with Agile sprints during some of the design and development phase.

Before your brain explodes, let's have a look at the Agile guiding principles.

Agile Guiding Principles

1. Our highest priority is to satisfy the customer through early and continuous delivery of valuable software.
2. Welcome changing requirements, even late in development. Agile processes harness change for the customer's competitive advantage.
3. Deliver working software frequently, from a couple of weeks to a couple of months, with a preference to the starter timescale.
4. Business people and developers must work together throughout the project.
5. Build projects around motivated individuals. Give them

the environment and support they need, and trust them to get the job done.

6. The most efficient and effective method of conveying information to and within a development team is face-to-face conversation.

7. Working software is the primary measure of progress.

8. Agile processes promote sustainable development. The sponsors, developers, and users should be able to maintain a constant pace indefinitely.

9. Continuous attention to technical excellence and good design enhances agility.

10. Simplicity—the art of maximising the amount of work not done—is essential.

11. The best architectures, requirements, and designs emerge from self-organising teams.

12. At regular intervals, the team reflects on how to become more effective, then tunes and adjusts its behaviour accordingly.

I'm sorry if your brain just exploded halfway through this list. There is a lot to take in, but we're not going to get into the detail of all of it here. There are loads of books and courses that will train you in great detail how to be an Agile Project Manager. If that's what you want.

But not this one!

Our purpose here is to give you a taste and explain what you need to know when you are on the fringes of project world. And, let's be honest, there are lots of great principles in there that we can apply to any project, whether it's Agile or not.

Such as the belief that the customer is king and needs to be involved in the whole project.

Yes! Always!

Don't waste time doing stuff that's not needed. Yes! This is one of the guiding principles of my life. Especially when applied to things that aren't fun. Like housework! And ironing socks.

Another thing I love about these values is the element of trusting the team. Project teams must be given the tools, skills, training, and trust to be able to do their jobs, experiment, fail, learn, and develop. Yes, they must receive all of these things. Except Fred. He is a lost cause. But everyone else should have all of this.

That's all great, but how do we actually apply all of it in the real world?

Well, let's assume that we are applying Agile principles to the design and development phase of a standard waterfall project.

We take baby steps...

For example, we will still do our requirements gathering to understand what needs to be delivered in terms of user or customer outcomes. We will just do it in a different way.

Bear with me, it will become clearer...

The Agile process is broken up into a series of iterations. An iteration will address a specific problem or desired outcome, and develop part of the overall product. Each iteration is comprised of the following activities, and is usually given a specific time period, e.g. thirty days:

- Planning
- Analysis
- Design
- Coding
- Testing
- Development

In planning, we create the team structure for this piece of the work. They agree how they will work together, with the focus being on trust, communication, and on solving the problem, rather than producing a lot of documentation.

The aim of this activity is to define the problem and generate *user stories*. The main difference between this approach and waterfall planning is that, rather than just attempting to organise activities, the Agile planning process is focused on solving problems.

In analysis, it's all about looking at the problems to be solved. Then figuring out what will be built, why it's being built, how long it might take, and in what order to do the work.

This analysis generates estimates, as well as a lot of output, called *artefacts*, such as system proposals, documents, templates, and spreadsheets, which will support later sprints.

In design, we begin to make high-level decisions to define the software architecture. Developers work closely with the users or customers to design and test their proposals.

The code is then written, and it's tested as it's being written. The Agile testing phase is different from the waterfall approach in this regard. With waterfall, everything is tested together when all of the design and development work is finished. In Agile, we test as we go along, then do some user testing at the end of each sprint. This provides great and immediate customer feedback, which generates the production of functional code rather than a written description of test results.

Finally, we get to the highly iterative development stage where we conduct final testing, carry out any necessary rework, complete the documentation for the final version of the system and for training purposes, and then we are ready to launch into the live environment.

After each iteration, there will be a *sprint review meeting* where the work that has been done is presented to stakeholders to demonstrate the value added and obtain their feedback. This allows plans and iterations to be changed rapidly if needed, based on the feedback received.

A *retrospective meeting* then takes place, which allows the team to think about how well they worked together, and what they could do better next time. They may follow the *start/stop/continue model* for this discussion, outlining what things they should *start* doing in the next iteration, what they should *stop* doing, and what worked well and should *continue*.

Throughout all of this activity, there will be the infamous *daily stand-up meetings*. For those readers who are new to project management and to Agile, this is the one aspect of Agile project management that you may have heard of.

This is just a bunch of project people standing around making jokes every morning, then? That doesn't sound very efficient.

Well, actually, there may be some jokes, us Project Managers do think we are hilarious, and we do love a captive audience. But, unfortunately, there is a serious element to these meetings as well.

The team will meet every day for around fifteen minutes, usually first thing in the morning, to give a status update on:

- What I did yesterday
- What I am doing today
- What is in my way

So, not much time for jokes! It's an efficient way of communicating, making sure everyone is on the same page, and that obstacles are quickly identified and removed. And, as we have already seen, communication is king in the Agile world with its emphasis on 'show, don't tell', working software vs lengthy documentation.

And this is another thing I love about the Agile way—the approach to meetings. They need to be short, focused, productive, and should only include the people who will benefit from being in them.

If I had my way, every business meeting would be like this. And scheduled for fifteen minutes! Let's cut the waffle and get to the point!

Which leads nicely onto the next bit of terminology that you may be familiar with—the *Scrum*™!

Scrum™ Methodology

Scrum™[3] what? Erm, isn't that something that rugby players do? Do we really have time to be throwing a ball around right in the middle of our project?

We definitely do not, as we are embarking on one of the most time-focused methodologies in project management, where every second counts!

The Scrum™ methodology was one of the foundations for developing the Agile approach to project management.

Confused much? Stay with me. We are getting there...

Scrum™ teams have three key roles. Firstly, we have the *Scrum*™ *Master*, responsible for coaching the team on *Scrum*™ *principles* to achieve the necessary behaviour changes required for Agile, and for embedding these into the organisation. They also organise the Scrum™ process and will undertake some reporting.

---

[3] Scrum™™ (the Agile methodology) is a trademark of Jeff Sutherland

Then, we have the *Product Owner*, representing everyone who has a stake in the project and its output. They organise project funding and prioritise the work to get the best value for the effort, prioritising the backlog, refining work items, clarifying needs with stakeholders, and agreeing to measures of success.

Then we have the *Scrum™ Team,* a multi-skilled, self-organising build or development team, consisting of different roles/skills needed on the project, e.g., developers. These people are responsible for converting the *product backlog* to achieving *increments of functionality* through a 24-hour interaction. Erm, what now?

The product backlog is the list of tasks that the team needs to complete, the 'to do list', if you like. Increment of functionality is any type of functionality which adds to the achievement of the overall project goal. An improvement on the previous version.

And we have some Scrum™ principles, yes? Of course. Any project methodology worth its salt must have a set of principles! The Scrum™ principles are:

1. *Empirical process control* - it's all about transparency, inspection and adaptation.
2. *Self-organisation* - team members with unlimited access to information, tools, and training who can organise themselves will be more creative and innovative.
3. *Collaboration* - awareness, articulation, appropriation creates great communication and better interaction.
4. *Value-based prioritisation* - focus on delivering maximum business value as soon as possible.

5. *Time-boxing* - in Scrum™ time is seen as the limiting constraint and must be used wisely. Meetings have specific time limits.
6. *Iterative development* - adapt, improve, repeat.

And these principles are adhered to in the various Scrum™ meetings:

- Sprint planning - prioritising the backlog
- Daily Scrum™ meetings - similar to the Agile daily stand-up meeting
- Sprint review - presenting what's been developed
- Sprint retrospective - a lessons learned session before the next sprint planning meeting

The Scrum™ approach works well where the people involved understand their role and the guiding principles, and they have the freedom to make decisions and organise themselves. It is highly suited to iterative system development work, but can often fail when applied to other project types, especially in traditionally hierarchical organisations where every decision has to be approved by 'someone higher up'.

These, again, are just the basics to introduce you to some of the terminology.

But now let's look at another methodology used in the Agile project world, which focuses on production rather than time as the key constraint—Kanban!

Kanban

Kanban is another Agile system, this time focused around efficiency production. Rather than roles and meetings, everything here relates to the *Kanban Board*. If you love a nice whiteboard, coloured pens, and sticky notes, then you're going to love this!

Imagine the whiteboard divided into six columns each relating to a stage of the project or production process.

In their simplest form, column headings can be:

- To do
- Doing
- Done

but can include more headings, such as:

- Tasks/Backlog/Stories/Problems
- In Progress
- Blocked*
- Peer Review
- Testing
- Done

*Blocked is not really a typical Kanban term. It should really be in the 'in progress' section, but I have seen it added for greater transparency.

Each sticky note represents a task to be completed, and it moves across the board depending on the stage it's at. Team members 'pull' a task and work on it until it hits the 'Done' column. They can't pull another task until they finish the one they are working on. Simple!

I love this approach, because I like to keep things simple, and a visual representation like this really works for me. It's so much easier to understand the state of play on a project when you can see the whole thing in front of you, rather than wading through pages of Gantt charts.

And if the visual isn't enough, there are various measures that are used to demonstrate the flow of work and efficiency:

- Throughput - the total number of tasks completed in a specific time frame
- Lead time - time taken from appearing on the board to 'Done'
- Cycle time - time spent in the 'In progress' section
- Blocked time - how long the tasks spend in the 'Blocked' section

By understanding and addressing the root cause of any delays in the process, the team can become increasingly more efficient. If you have a lot of items stuck in 'Peer review', for example, then you can investigate why that is and do something about it.

So, there we have it, a quick guide to the essentials of Agile project management. As I said at the beginning of this chapter, I've included it because I see organisations attempting to apply it more and more outside of the software development arena. It's very different from the waterfall approach, and many organisations are now trying to create a hybrid project management approach that incorporates the best of both methodologies. This does create a challenge in finding suitably qualified and experienced Project Managers, as the skillsets are very different, and not many can do both approaches well. It's also quite difficult to scale for very complex transformation programmes beyond three or four teams of between five and nine people, as it becomes very difficult to manage.

But, for Agile methods to work, the organisation needs to be ready as a whole, to understand what Agile means, even at a high level, and to have the culture in place to support it. You can try to limit it to the IT and Change/Project functions, but that's to deny how Agile is supposed to work. You've immediately excluded the people in Marketing, Sales, and Service Operations, who would be your product owners or team members.

If it's not rolled out properly, there's a risk that it's seen as the latest fad, and the 'not invented here' brigade will rail against it if they don't know what it is and haven't been involved in its adoption.

The adoption of any new methodology needs to be planned, and it needs to be supported by the senior management of the organisation. The idea of adopting it needs to be rolled out in the same way as if we were launching a new product—with change management principles!

Remember everything we learned about business readiness in Chapter 6? If you are going to attempt to change your entire organisation to adopt Agile principles, then you need to treat the launch of this as a new project!

The future of software development will be reliant on the Agile approach for some time to come. Until something else comes along that replaces it with the promise of faster, cheaper, more successful, and so on. The world demands problems be solved faster, companies be more innovative, the customer's every whim be catered to.

For now, for those of you who are on the periphery of project world, it makes sense to at least understand what it's about and how you can start to use some of the guiding principles in your day-to-day job.

With the number of companies who are recruiting Agile experts at the time of writing, I'm quite sure it won't be too long before someone comes along and asks you to be part of an Agile project team!

Chapter 11 Summary - What Have We Learned?

- What the Agile project management methodology is and how it differs from waterfall
- The values and guiding principles of the Agile approach
- The Scrum™ and Kanban approaches and how they support Agile projects
- What to consider before adopting the Agile approach in your organisation

12

Bonus Section - Change Behaviours

Over the years I have become a bit of an expert at assessing what I call 'change behaviours'. Patterns of behaviour that I see regularly in project world. Regardless of city, company culture, organisation type, or time of day, they always pop up in some shape or form.

You might find this bit insightful. Or hilarious. Or even a bit, yeah, so what-ish?

But the truth of the matter is that, for the uninitiated, or the new Project Managers, these are the things that can derail them. Not the project itself, but behaviours that pop up during a project that can affect them personally.

There are definitely easier ways to make a living than running projects. But those of us who choose to do it, do so because we are a little bit addicted to bringing order to chaos, fixing problems, and firefighting. It's all adrenaline-inducing stuff. And it requires a thick skin, resilience, and strength of character to survive, and to flourish, in such a crazy world.

To help prepare you for some of it and help you to not just *survive* your first project, but also to hopefully enjoy it, here are a few insights.

Knowledge Shaming

This is one of the things that prompted this book. Shaming people at work because they don't know everything you think they should know. Or because they don't know as much as you. Unfortunately, we all do it. People make mistakes, and it often annoys the rest of us.

How many of you have been annoyed by some poor call centre person who doesn't understand your problem or know how to fix it?

We all know, in the back of our minds, that this poor person being subjected to our impatience is possibly working in a second language, has only been trained on one aspect of the service, and is following a script. But it doesn't stop us being annoyed at them.

It's the same thing in project world. Someone has been drafted in to work on a project, and they have no idea what's going on, how things work, or what half of the jargon means.

Early on in my career, I was quite impatient. I thought everyone knew more than me about what we were trying to do, and when they didn't do it as quickly as I wanted, or in the way that I wanted, I would get quite frustrated. Rather than take it out on the individual concerned, though, I would bottle it up and just get more stressed about the situation.

Nowadays, thankfully, I am better equipped to deal with these situations. I have realised over the years that, just because someone has a shiny, new project management certificate, it doesn't mean that they are going to know how to do everything perfectly from day one. Or, because they have been in a work environment for a number of years, that they are familiar with, or have been exposed to, all of the same things as me. So, I make fewer assumptions, and I ask more questions.

And I firmly believe that 50% of project management is learning the tools and the jargon, and the other 50% is learning the skills that are needed to make stuff happen and resolve problems. And that only comes from experience.

Let's not do the knowledge-shaming thing, calling people out or rolling our eyes because they 'don't get it'.

Let's encourage the 'stupid questions', and the experience sharing, and avoid people worrying themselves sick because they don't understand what their boss wants from them.

Or worse, saying that they are doing the work and then missing the deadline. Because they don't know where to start.

And the reverse is also true. If you have someone older and wiser in your team, you can be sure they have encountered whatever situation is troubling you at least once in their career. Use their knowledge. Why repeat the same mistakes they had to learn the hard way?

Speak up, people. You don't need to do it in public, but go and have a quick word with your boss or a colleague, and just ask them. You don't need to plead complete ignorance of the subject. You can do it in a way that shows your interest in learning, without looking like a complete numpty. For example:

"I'm really interested in what you were saying about xyz. Would you have ten minutes to talk me through it in more detail?"

I can guarantee that any Change Leader or Head of Projects worth their salt will be doing cartwheels inside. Why? Because we love nothing more than talking about change stuff and sharing what we know. Trust me, ask. You will make their day!

Conflict Resolution & Influencing Skills

Every project job ad asks for excellent influencing skills. But what does that mean?

Someone who can bend spoons with their mind? A manipulative, Machiavellian genius who can make others do their bidding without them realising? Or a people pleaser, who tries to make everyone happy, but doesn't actually deliver the project?

For me, it's someone who can get agreement on points of disagreement or friction between the project team, or between the project and stakeholders. It's not really about influencing. It's about listening to the people on either side. If they feel heard, and you understand their end game, i.e., what they want/what they are worried about, then you are halfway there.

If you can put those concerns to the other party and share a different perspective, then barriers start to come down, and reconciliation is possible. And win-win situations can be achieved.

But how does that work in projects?

Managing large, complex projects can be stressful. Managing people can be a challenge. Managing the two things together, under pressure, with senior management looking over your shoulder, can be overwhelming.

Throw in a bit of change resistance, a couple of people working on the project who don't really want to be there, and a stakeholder or two who want things done their way or the highway.

A perfect recipe for a bit of conflict, no?

Some Project Managers cope by developing a somewhat dry (some might say cynical) sense of humour. I might be one of those.

Others drink wine (ok, that may also be me).

Some take to the gym for vigorous workouts (that's not me).

And some go home and yell at their long-suffering partners (I try not to do that to the person who cooks my delicious dinners. And buys my wine).

However, I have discovered a couple of methods that are more effective.

The first is diffusing the situation before it becomes a thing. Technically, it's called conflict resolution. I was so fascinated by how powerful people's feelings in conflict situations were, that I went off to the wonderful school of law at Strathclyde University to study it in more detail.

And here is what I learned. If you can take the time to understand the feelings of both parties on either side of a conflict, and make those feelings known to each of them, then you are a long way towards fixing the situation.

If the parties are able to see the situation from the other person's perspective, and to understand what that person is worried about, then you have a great chance of fixing it.

If both parties are then able to articulate what they need from the situation and can find a way to help each other get what they need then, job done, you've cracked it.

Instead of two people facing each other head on, if you can have them standing side by side, looking at the problem together, the focus suddenly shifts from trying to prove each other wrong to 'how do we fix this?'.

For example, say we have Susan, who is refusing to budge on some system configuration requests. She wants them done her way.

Joe, the developer, has built the system in a slightly different way, based on the information he had at the time. He is refusing to make the changes, as he doesn't have enough time and doesn't think they are important.

By explaining to him what Susan is worried about and why, Joe is better able to understand why Susan is making her 'demands'. By asking Joe how he thinks we can meet Susan's needs, perhaps in a different or more creative way, you are making the developer part of the solution. And they begin to feel less defensive. Most people want to be helpful. Nobody goes to work in the morning determined to be unhelpful.

The developer is then able to come up with an alternative approach to address Susan's concerns, and everyone is happy. All it takes is one person prepared to open up initially, making themselves a little bit vulnerable, and then, by saying what they need, they can transform an otherwise tricky situation.

However, if either party is just being bloody-minded, then a quick chat about how their attitude isn't helpful ought to do the trick. And, if not, then sometimes we need to escalate to their manager to ask for help in tackling the situation. But this is always a last resort, as nobody wants to be a tattletale!

The second great stress reducer is working for (and with) people who understand the need for a little vent. They let you into their office, listen carefully while you rant about the injustices of the situation, make soothing noises, then happily let you wander off without actually having said anything of any substance. Those people know who they are. Thank you for listening. And for continuing to let me in to your now 'virtual' offices.

Keep it Simple

Another pet hate is people overcomplicating things. Stop laughing! The irony of this from a consultant, yes, I know... Ok, I get it...it's funny.

But it's true. I believe that a true expert is someone who can explain something in a really simple way that anyone can understand. Let's take a moment here to celebrate the legend that is David Attenborough. Very few of us are natural history experts. We haven't studied zoology or spent nights staring into the darkness through night vision goggles looking for the greater spotted lima bird (I don't think this bird actually exists, before anyone looks it up). But he has. He has devoted his whole life to it. And he is clearly an expert.

But his true gift is not that he is a brilliant scholar. His true gift is being able to share all of that knowledge in a way that we can all understand it. And not just understand. We are mesmerised by his wisdom. And his calm, soothing voice. He is a true expert.

At the other extreme, we have those I like to call 'content light'. Now, before you remind me what I said about knowledge-shaming above, let me just be clear. There is a difference in not knowing stuff and owning up to it and those who pretend they know stuff, or who know *some* stuff, but go to great lengths to make it sound super complicated for their own benefit.

Sometimes people speak in jargon to demonstrate how clever they are, or because they want to feel superior by making other people feel less clever. I find this very annoying. Sometimes they want to make something sound super complicated because they are trying to sell you the answer to your supposed problem. I also find this very annoying. Consultants do this sometimes by providing lengthy Powerpoint presentations that could actually be cut down to three or four pages. I try not to be one of those.

I once worked for someone, a very famous UK bank CEO, who said that if you couldn't get the whole story across in less than ten slides, then you didn't know what you were doing. I think he may have had a point.

The whole purpose of this book was to demystify project and project jargon, to make it less scary, to make it more accessible to everyone. Not just the people who are working in project world, but all of the people who are on the receiving end of change, or unwittingly seconded onto a project.

If I have achieved that in this book, then I will be very happy. If I haven't, and you still have questions, I will be more than happy to answer them over at thecactusclub.online.

Thanks for reading my book and good luck in all of your project-related endeavours!

Lesley Elder, April 2021

P.S. Any inaccuracies, spelling mistakes, or other errors in this book are down to Fred. I apologise on his behalf. I will be firing him shortly. Probably.

13

Acronyms

ACRONYMS

ADKAR	The ADKAR® model of change
ARIADD	The assumptions, risks, issues, actions, decisions and dependencies log
BRD	Business requirements document
CIA	Change Impact Assessment
COO	Chief Operating Officer
HR	Human Resources
HoC	Head of Change
FTE	Full time equivalent, used when counting the number of employees
KPI	Key performance indicator
KSC	Key success criteria
PIB	Project initiation board
PID	Project initiation document
PM	Project Manager
PMO	Project management office
PMP	Project management plan
PSG	Project steering group
PV	Planned value
RACI	Responsible, Accountable, Consulted, Informed
RAM	Responsibility assignment matrix
SME	Subject matter expert
SOW	Statement of work
TOM	Target operating model
WBS	Work breakdown structure

14

Glossary

Actions
  Activities noted at project meetings

Adoption Cycle
  How quickly people are likely to embrace a new idea/product

Agile
  A project management methodology

Assumptions
  Points that need to be confirmed and added to the RAID or ARIADD log

Benefits
  What will be achieved if the project is completed

Budget
  The funding for the project

Burn Rate
  The rate at which the project is spending money

Business Case
  The document which shows the costs and benefits of the project

Business Mobilisation
  The activities required to get the business ready for the change

Business Readiness
  The activities required to get the business ready for the change

Business Requirements
  What the project needs to address to deliver the benefits

Cost Centre
  Where project costs are allocated to in the finance system

Change Champion
  A business representative who promotes the change

Change CurveR
  The Kubler-Ross model of explaining reaction to change

Change Impact Assessment
  A process for identifying business areas impacted by the change

Change Fatigue
The effect of delivering lots of change to one business area

Change Request
A project governance process asking for permission to increase budget or delay delivery

Contingency Plan
The course of action if the initial implementation fails

Cost Plan
A forecast of planned project spend over a period of time

Critical Path
The 'must do' project activities which take the longest time to complete

Data Dictionary
A document which indicates the data standards and norms for the project

Decisions
Items recorded at project meetings and added to the RAID or ARIADD log

Dependencies
Project activities which are dependent on completion of another activity

Delegated Authority
The level of authority for decisions, usually related to finan-

cial approval limits

Gantt Chart
A project plan showing milestones and duration of the project

Governance Process
The framework for managing the project.

Intangible Benefit
Usually a non-monetary value benefit of completing a project

Issue
An item that could cause a problem for delivery of the project

Kanban
An Agile project methodology

Key Person Risk
A project dependency on a single person for a specific piece of work or provide expertise

Key Performance Indicator
Measures of the project performance

Kick-off Workshop
The initial meeting of the project team

Lessons Learned Log
Items learned during the course of the project which could assist future project teams

Migration Risk Report

A document highlighting any increased risk during the project implementation phase

Milestone

A key project deliverable

Pet Projects

An initiative supported by a manager for his or her own benefit or interest

Plan

The collection of activities required to complete the project

Planning Workshop

A project team meeting to develop the plan

Project Board

The group responsible for assessing project progress and making decisions

Project Charter

The document stating the project purpose, key deliverables and scope of the work

Project Management Plan

The document which states how the work will be delivered

Project Lifecycle

The five stages of projects from initiation to planning, execution, testing and closure

Project Portfolio
  An organisation's projects

Project Scope
  What the project will and will not deliver

Project Sponsor
  The business manager responsible for leading the project and realising the benefits

Project Steering Group
  See project board

Process Map
  A step-by-step outline of the activities in a business process

Proof of Concept
  An initial trial of the project on a small sample, eg one business area or location

Prosci®
  Company responsible for developing the ADKAR® change management methodology

RACI Matrix
  A table to show who is responsible, accountable, consulted and informed on projects

RAID Log
  A document containing project risks, assumptions, issues, and dependencies

Regulatory Project
A project required to implement changes necessary for regulatory or legal compliance

Release Management Approach
The scheduling process for projects, usually relating to IT

Release Schedule
The plan for implementation of projects into the organisation

Responsibility Assessment Matrix
A table showing who will do what on the project team

Resource Plan
Shows which resources are allocated to the project and when they will be required

Return on Investment
The amount of profit or benefit expected from investment

Risk
Something that could negatively impact the project in the future

Roadmap
A timeline which shows when projects and activities will impact the organisation

Scope Creep
Additional activities or requirements that were not originally planned

Scrum^{TM}
An Agile project methodology

Sparkly Unicorn
Something used to distract someone requesting additional project deliverables

Sprint
A short period when a Scrum^{TM} team works to complete a set amount of activity

Stage Gate
A decision point on the project, part of the governance process

Stakeholder
Someone who has an interest in the outcome of the project or is impacted by the change

Stakeholder Map
A tool for showing the level of knowledge, engagement, power or influence of project stakeholders

Statement of Work
Similar to a contract, outlining the work to be completed by an individual or supplier

Status Report
A regular report stating project progress, highlighting risks and issues and the costs

Strategic Fit

Determining whether a project is aligned with the overall strategy of the business

Success Criteria
Activities specified by the business for successful delivery of the project

Tangible Benefit
An outcome of delivering the project, usually with a financial value

Waterfall Approach
A sequential project methodology

Work Package
A set of project activities leading to completion of a milestone